Standing Firm on Feet of Clay

…from broken to healing to whole

Acknowledgements

Every single person that breathed a prayer for my family, I thank you.

Tina, Lynette and Kim, thank you for your formatting, organizing and editing skills. I really appreciate your friendships and your willingness to help a girl.

Thank you to Sarah and Shannon at Socially Seasoned. Our meetings have yet to feel like work. Your brains impress me.

Cheryl, your wisdom, patience, encouragement and perspective will always be appreciated by me. I sincerely thank you.

Thank you, Pastor Jim, for your guidance and love for us. You are so appreciated and incredibly missed.

Rocky, thank you for your guidance, insight and commitment to Brian and our family.

Aunt Marianne, thank you for praying for me, standing strong with me and loving me. You know a whole lot more than nothing.

Char, Debi and Suzette, there is no way to put into words what your friendships mean to me. Your love for me, regardless of my state of mind, is so undeserved yet so appreciated. Thank you for burning up the lines to heaven with your prayers. Thank you for breakfasts that turn into lunches. Thank you for the laughter that draws stares. I love you, my soul sisters.

Neil and Von, thank you for raising my husband strong and loving. Thank you for pointing him to the cross. I love you both.

Judi, I really hit the jackpot in the sister department. Thank you for being my gatekeeper. I love you.

Dad, I love you. Thank you for our morning phone calls. Thank you for the firm foundation you and mom modeled for me. Thank you for your prayers, your strength and your endless encouragement and for laughing at my jokes.

Sidney, Keaton, and Trenton (Surely, Goodness and Mercy,) you three are the most amazing kids ever. Your humor, laughter, determination, positive perspectives, and hugs on demand are my fuel. Your growth, maturity and faith astound me. You are hemmed in.

Brian, you are so worth it. I love you.

"Every time I think of you, I give thanks to my God." Philippians 1:3 NLT

1

Lord, I believe you want me to write this book. I believe you are calling me to do this to help other people who are faced with a similar situation. I believe you will give me the words and equip me with wisdom. I'm scared and doubtful, but know you have called me to this.

Ephesians 3:20-21

"Now to Him who is able to do immeasurably more than all we ask or imagine, according to His power that is at work within us, to Him be glory in the church and in Christ Jesus throughout all generations, forever and ever! Amen."

I, Jill, take you, Brian, to be my Husband. To have and to hold, from this day forward. For better, for worse, for richer, for poorer, in sickness and in health. To love and to cherish, for as long as we both shall live. This is my solemn vow.

I remember this day so well. I remember waking up in my twin bed in my childhood bedroom that morning at six and getting in the shower. My stomach was in knots and I was super nervous. I couldn't believe that I would be Mrs. Brian Clay by the end of the day. I went from giddy laughter to stomach flips back to giddy laughter in a matter of seconds. I stood in that shower and told myself that I would stand there until my nerves were settled and then get on with this once in a lifetime day. Brian is an amazing man. He makes me laugh like no one else. He is strong in his beliefs. He is spontaneous and fun. I didn't want to live life without him. I kept telling myself that after this amazing day I was leaving on vacation with the man of my dreams!

I put my make up on and put hot rollers in my hair... hey, it was the early 90s, lay off! My mom and I were going to go to the church together and everyone else would meet us there. On the way we stopped at McDonalds for a large Coke...a drink I still crave to this day. We arrived at the church and started getting ready. The flowers had already been delivered, and the photographer arrived shortly after we did. Months of planning this day and things were falling into place.

Brian and I decided to not see each other before the ceremony, so he and his groomsmen got dressed and had their pictures taken first because, well, aside from figuring out the tux button covers, their job was pretty easy.

Then it was my turn for pictures. I remember posing for a long time with my parents, along with my sister who was my maid of honor and all my sweet bridesmaids! We laughed and cried and then laughed because we cried. While in the sanctuary we heard Brian and his groomsmen in the church gym that was located under the sanctuary. They were playing basketball in their tuxedos and having a blast. I was just hoping that Brian didn't break his nose or lose any teeth 30 minutes before the ceremony.

Then we were ushered away into the Bridal room off of the sanctuary to wait for the ceremony to start. Our pastor came in with the marriage license and had me sign it. Brian had already signed it that morning. Yikes! When I saw his signature on that certificate the stomach flips started again. This was really happening. This is as real as it gets! We were diving into the unknown waters of marriage and a committed life together. Wow! We really didn't know much back then, but praise God we serve a mighty God who would lead us through it all.

Then, I was standing at the back of the church with my dad. All the bridesmaids had made it to their places at the front of the sanctuary. All the groomsmen were up there standing with my Groom. I took my dad's arm and said, "I can't feel my legs." He said, "Well, hang on because we are going in!" The wedding march started, the doors opened, when everyone stood in that packed church and down the aisle we went.

Brian told me later that I was smiling so big that he couldn't see my eyes. My dad gave me away and the ceremony started. At one point as a song was being sung I was asking Brian if he won the basketball game down stairs. We were laughing and talking and then as the song ended, the pastor said, "Well, I can honestly say that I've never had to interrupt a couple to marry them before." I'm so glad we have the wedding on tape so I can watch it occasionally and enjoy those moments again.

Our reception was at a golf club and the place was gorgeous. It had been a very rainy summer and August 1st was literally the first Saturday we had sunshine all day. My sister caught my bouquet and later in that month she went on a blind date and met her future husband. They were married 11 months later. One of Brian's groomsmen caught the garter and was married a year after our wedding. All in all, I always felt that God had blessed our relationship, our wedding day and our marriage.

2

Love is a decision. I make a choice to love each day. Yes. It's glorious to have the warm fuzzies, those tingly feelings that we get when we are attracted to someone and sparks start to fly, but those are truly just feelings. That emotion doesn't stick around. Feelings ebb and flow. Happiness ebbs and flows. Sorrow ebbs and flows. I made a decision to love in good times and in bad, in stable times and scary times, as well as in laughter and in anger. I chose to love in brokenness and despair, in joyful times and in prosperous times.

When Brian and I were dating and then became engaged, we joked about anything and everything. We did, however, make a firm "off limits" stand on joking about divorce. We knew once we started joking about it, then it could become more acceptable in our minds and conversations and even perhaps become an option. We chose not to joke about divorce.

I will never forget overhearing a heated phone conversation at work once between a man and his ex-wife. He screamed, yelled and cursed, thinking that because his door was closed no one could hear…. Or not caring who could hear. Another man, who overheard as well, said to me in passing, "You can end a marriage, but divorce goes on forever."

On a typical and ordinary day, my perspective of the world, my life and my future was shattered. I could have done it. I could have divorced Brian. I would have made it through with God's grace. But that wasn't what God had in mind for me or my family. God had a different plan. He asked me to follow, and I stepped out in faith, not knowing what that would look like.

People have asked me, "How?" "How did you do it?" "How did you stay?"

My honest answer is that I really don't know, except for the grace of God. There were struggles each day. There are still struggles. Daily, hourly, sometimes literally by the minute calling on God to comfort, guide, take over my words, take over my responses, and make the doubts leave my mind. Calling on Him for strength, this is the way we should live every day as Christians and being in that pit put my reliance on Him. I was working on healing. Healing myself, healing my marriage, and helping my kids heal.

3

September 2, 2011
Labor Day Weekend

The day was like any other day in the call center. Hundreds of calls come in each day. I was attached to the phone, and held to a rigid schedule. About 12:10 I get a call from the security desk that my husband is at the door downstairs. I don't have time for this -- he knows how demanding my job is. I log out, and run down the stairs. "What's going on?" I ask my husband.

"The kids are fine, but I need to tell you something," he says.

He pulls me outside as if the security guard shouldn't hear what he has to say. He backs me up against a pillar of the building and says, "There are accusations at the church that I'm having an affair." My immediate answer was, "Who do we need to talk to in order to get this cleared up?"

Brian explains that our pastor, Jim Pearson, is in the parking lot around the corner, and that I need to leave work to come with him. I'm arguing with him. I can't leave work – it's the middle of the day! He insists, so we head upstairs and tell my manager that I have a family emergency, (way more than I knew), and that I need to leave.

We walk to my car and Brian is strangely quiet. We hike across the street. Silence. Up three flights of stairs in a parking garage. Silence. Looking back, I should have been prepared, but one can never be fully prepared for what was about to come. As we get near to the car, he asks if I want him to drive. I say, "No. I can drive my own car." He sits in the passenger seat and as I'm starting the car he says, "The accusations are true." At that moment it's too much to handle. I get out of the car and tell him he's driving.

I remember crying… or maybe more like moaning, they were odd sounds that didn't register as they were coming from my own body. I remember a million thoughts flooding my mind, but I couldn't put the pieces together. I could not form words. I remember staring at him, probably with my mouth hanging open in shock. I remember after a while saying, "No," very quietly and then "No," a little louder and then a little louder until I was probably screaming.

The two of us drove to the parking lot where Pastor Jim was waiting in Brian's car. I remember staring at nothing while occasionally crying out. I don't remember the words I used. They probably weren't words at all. I didn't want to look at Brian, but I was unable to look away.

Pastor Jim got into my car with us and said, "Tell me what's going on, Brian."

On that hot September day, crowded in our car, Brian squirmed and didn't tell us much. He said that he had met this woman and had "an encounter" with her but it wasn't sex. Pastor Jim said, "Brian it was sex, don't dance around this." Brian said, "Yes, but only once." We found out later that it was sex on three different occasions. He was slow to admit it as if he could lessen the damage or dampen the pain. "You sound like Bill Clinton," I remember saying, as Brian was giving us half-truths and half-baked stories.

Pastor Jim explained to me at this point that he had gotten a voicemail that morning from someone claiming a woman had confessed to her that she was having an affair with Brian. Brian and Pastor Jim already had a pre-arranged meeting that morning to discuss the upcoming weekend service. Brian frequently preached when Pastor Jim went out of town on vacation, and this holiday weekend was no exception. When Brian arrived for the meeting, Jim confronted him about the call. Brian just said, "We need to go get Jill." We lived in a close-knit community with school and church groups overlapping. Pastor Jim had already received word that calls were beginning to come into the church. The news was spreading like wildfire. When I heard that news, I knew I had to go get our kids immediately. This was probably just my need to have them near me. I did not want them to hear anything from anyone but us. First, however, Brian needed to tell his parents, Neil and Von, before they heard the horrific story from someone else.

I insisted on being there when he told them partly because I didn't want him to sugar coat or downplay it and partly because I needed to hear it again to see if it made any more sense by hearing it a second time. Brian drove his car while Jim drove my car, again with me as a passenger. While Jim drove, I called my sister and my dad and told them what limited things I knew and that they needed to be praying because I didn't know what was going to happen. My life had just turned upside down.

4

My relationship with my in-laws had always been uneasy. It was my first rodeo with in-laws and their first rodeo with a daughter-in-law. We had a series of misunderstandings and poor communication that had just built up over the years. I always knew it could be better. I *wanted* it to be better!

As Brian, Jim and I went into my in-laws' home, Brian got right to the point. After hearing Brian's words, his father came to me and hugged me. I think I collapsed, and we ended up on the floor crying. I felt numb and Neil just held me. Brian's mom, Von, in the meantime, began yelling. She directed her anger at Brian, asking, *"WHY?"* Over and over. At some point, she ran to the bathroom and got sick.

Brian said he was going to get some of his things out of the house to sleep somewhere else. I don't think he could listen to his mom getting sick and his dad and me crying any longer. He got up quickly and said, "I'm going to get some stuff out of the house and find somewhere to sleep tonight." His parents wanted him to sleep at their house and he said, "No." I don't really know why, except that he had hurt them so terribly with this. And he probably didn't want to see their pain. Neil and Pastor Jim followed him not wanting him to be alone, not sure what he was capable of at this point. Von called Carin, Brian's sister in Illinois, to tell her what was happening. Von and I told her together what we knew at this point. She was already planning to come to Fort Wayne that weekend since it was Labor Day Weekend. It was certainly not the Labor Day weekend any of us had planned.

With the rumor mill starting to spin like crazy, and the church getting phone calls questioning what was happening, I became focused on one thing: I wanted to get the kids from school before they heard this from someone else. I knew that no one would be vicious and blurt things out to the kids intentionally. At this point, however, I didn't know who, what, when, where, or why, and I wanted to make sure that they were protected from this news until we could tell them. At that moment, I needed them near me. I needed them with me.

I asked Von, my mother-in law, to go with me to get the kids from school. We picked up Trenton, our youngest son, first from the elementary school. I asked the receptionist to call and get him from class to come home early.

While we waited, Pastor Kelly Byrd, the Pastor of Blackhawk Ministries where the kids went to school walked into the lobby, and when Von saw him she broke down. He was Neil and Von's pastor and knew Brian and me through the school. Von stopped him in the lobby and explained to him that Brian had been unfaithful and we were picking up the kids from school. He pulled us into an empty office. It was actually the School Administrator's office. I cannot go into that office or that area of the school since that day without thinking of those moments.

I remember Pastor Byrd asked what we knew and between the two of us Von and I explained (probably not very clearly) what we knew at that point. He asked me if I still loved Brian. I said, "Yes." And then he prayed with us. Although Pastor Byrd didn't know the story and I'm sure we appeared completely out of sorts, he probably thought he had just walked into a tornado. It was a beautiful moment, a divine appointment, actually. None of us knew much of the details at the time, but his wisdom and kindness at that moment is something I will never forget. I will always appreciate Pastor Byrd's calming presence that day. I do not remember the words he spoke in prayer, but I remember the peace that passes all understanding that began to do its work to calm my heart.

I do remember being anxious to get to my kids. I was distracted, obviously, and wanted to hug my sweet kids. I didn't know what our lives would look like after that day.

Trenton was sitting in the lobby waiting for us. He looked scared not knowing why he was called out of school early. I told him everyone was okay, but we needed to get home and talk to Daddy.

We then drove with Trenton across the street to pick Sidney and Keaton up from the Jr./Sr. High School. The receptionist had called the Principal, Linda Pearson, who also happens to be Pastor Jim's wife to get the kids from their classes and bring them out to us. I parked and walked towards the school when Linda met me outside with Sidney and Keaton. I hugged the kids probably tight enough to hurt them and told them to get in the van and I would explain everything when we got home. Linda hugged me and told me she didn't know much, but that Jim had called her, devastated. She told me she loved us and was praying for our family.

We made the short trip home with the kids asking what in the world was going on. What they didn't know at the time is that I was just as clueless. I had no idea why Brian had an affair. I had no idea if he wanted to stay with me in our marriage. Who was this other woman? Did I know her? Did he love her? Was she destroying her family too? We all sat in the living room together, Brian, Sidney, Keaton, Trenton, Neil, Von, Pastor Jim and myself. Pastor Jim started talking when suddenly Brian blurted out, "I had an affair. I cheated on your mother."
Keaton was sitting on the arm of the couch and half on my lap with Trenton next to me on the couch… Keaton turned to me and said,

"You are going to forgive him, right Mom?" Looking at those big eyes, inches from my face, filling with tears I said, "I'm going to try."

Sidney's first response was anger. She was crying and mad. She literally wouldn't look at her dad or talk to him. This went on for days. Trenton was in tears. He was, as we all were, not sure what our lives would look like after this day. The security of his family was rocked, and shaken. He never left my side for long. He was and still is very tender hearted. Keaton was very sensitive as well, but he kept a lot of his feelings inside. He would try to make me laugh and let me tell you he's really good at it. They all tried to be comic relief, while we did a lot of hugging, praying together, and strangely enough, laughing.

The rock that Pastor Jim was to me and our family during this time is indescribable. He was prayerful, strong, forgiving and, frankly, Brian screwed up his holiday weekend as well. The calming effect he had on me and our family in that devastating time will never be forgotten.

5

After our conversation with the kids, Brian left. He stayed at a family friend's house that night. Sidney stayed with friends. The boys and I were home. I called my small group and asked them to come and pray with me. I remember asking them not to hate Brian…. Weird, I know. I somehow knew that if this turned into an "I hate Brian" tirade, it would take even longer to heal. I told them what I knew.

Brian had also been in contact with the men in the small group and they really stepped up to support, love and guide us through the weeds. They of course, had questions like: Did I know her? Does she go to our church? Is she married too? How long has this been going on? Was he framed? Did someone set him up to try to destroy his ministry? These were all really good questions to which I still didn't have any answers. This group of friends in our small group was like no other. They were there in the mud with us; praying with us and for us, listening to and encouraging us. They even brought medicine to help me sleep.

That night, after the longest day of my life, I went into our bedroom to change for bed. I walked into the closet and saw that Brian's side of our closet was nearly empty. I broke down again. I sat down on the edge the bed and just screamed out to God to tell me why. Why? How could Brian do this to me? I thought we were building a good life together. He was a teaching pastor for goodness sake. How was I going to do this? I had so many questions swirling around in my head. The closet was so empty. I didn't know if he was gone forever. Did I want him gone forever? I found out later that Brian thought I wouldn't want to see any of his belongings, so he took them all. His mom humorously told me later that if she had been in my shoes she would have insisted he take it all because she would have burned whatever was left on the front lawn.

After a few weeks passed, Brian started putting the pieces of this story together for me. About five months before the affair, Brian started meeting people online. I believe they were just conversations and flirtations at this point. He told me he was not feeling desired, loved, needed or wanted. I was crazy about him, but he didn't see it or feel it. He met this woman online and they realized they had actually gone to school together years before. They talked online on a dating website for many weeks.

Brian wanted to meet her in person, but was afraid of being seen with her in public because many people knew him. She was willing, so they decided to meet at our home one morning after the kids had gone to school and I had gone to work. They apparently had their cruel fun in our basement that morning. Then the next morning they met at her home and the next morning after that as well. After their third encounter, that evening she told a friend of hers about the affair. This friend then got in contact with Pastor Jim.

On that Friday morning, Pastor Jim got a voicemail regarding this affair, so when Brian came in to work with Jim on the sermon for the following Sunday, Jim asked Brian to explain what this voicemail meant. Was there an explanation? Was any of this false? When Jim confronted him, Brian simply said, "We need to go get Jill from work. I need to talk to her first."

6

Affairs, no matter what the circumstances, always shock many people. It has a ripple effect. A devastating effect. I am grateful that this other woman's family still doesn't know about the affair. Her family didn't go through the humility of the affair being public. She didn't have the shame of people knowing about her bad choices.

Most every woman would say, "Not MY husband." The thing about Brian is he had such integrity. If he had told me that he had not done this, I would have believed him. He was smart and his faith was strong, and when he preached it was with passion and wisdom and yes, integrity. I think many had put him on a pedestal, myself included.

The Tuesday before I found out about the affair, I got home from work and went down in the basement for something. I had such a weird feeling when I was down there. Everything was in its place and that just wasn't normal. First of all, our three kids played down there all the time. That was the purpose of our basement -- so the kids could play, watch cartoons and play video games.

So, going downstairs and seeing every pillow in its place on the couches and no fruit snack wrappers laying around was very strange.

I stood there just looking around trying to figure if I had somehow cleaned the basement in my sleep. It was an eerie, unsettling feeling. I shook off the strange feeling and went on with whatever I was doing.

I had found out that the first encounter with this woman was in my basement on that previous Tuesday. I didn't know this woman and still don't, but having my marriage violated was devastating enough. Having my home violated at the same time was more than I could handle. They apparently thought meeting in our home would save them from being recognized or seen together in public. There was sex for three days of meetings. I asked my counselor if she thought Brian was fulfilled in doing this. I remember her saying that she didn't think so because he kept going back to see if he would eventually be fulfilled. Brian did tell me later that there was no fulfillment. In fact, all he felt afterwards was disgust.

 It really was a double whammy to learn of my husband's sin in my safe place, my home. I told Brian I wanted the two couches out of the basement ASAP and that he would pay for new furniture. I did mention fumigation too, but that might have been going too far.

Several friends and family came over Saturday morning to move our two couches out of the basement and take them to be donated. I was going to Big Lots and getting new furniture. Brian's sister, Carin, said, "Big Lots? This calls for more like Ethan Allen, don't you think?"

The kids, Carin and I piled into the van and drove to Big Lots. While we made our purchase, we went from laughter to tears several times. It was a short visit to the store, but fraught with emotion. The music playing over the speakers while we looked at furniture was hilarious, actually. The first song I remember hearing was "Baby Come Back" and if that wasn't enough, Hi Infidelity's "I'm Gonna Keep On Lovin' You" came on next. I remember Carin saying to me, "We really need to get you home because I'm scared of what song might come on next."

That Saturday, my sister, Judi, drove into town. Brian was at the house when she came in and said, "I love you, Brian." I will never forget that first response to him. She showed him grace when it would have been reasonable for her to deck him. I was almost relieved that this was her response. If she had been hateful to him I somehow feel I would have tried to repair the situation as strange as that sounds. He deserved much worse than she gave him. She was my shield and gate keeper that weekend.

I remember sitting on the couch doing Sudoku puzzles while trying not to break down. The kids were so gentle with me. Sometimes they would just sit and hold my hand or put their head in my lap. I was trying to occupy my mind and my hands, but I would just end up staring at the puzzles. Many pages of that book were ruined because of my tears. Judi took my phone away from me so I'd quit responding to people. She kept making my bed when I'd try to climb back in it. She tried to make me eat, but I couldn't. I would literally choke and gag on food during those first days. She would answer the door when the numerous people stopped by to see me and show their concern. I really appreciated everybody's concern. Nobody knew what to do, especially me. I'm so grateful to my sister for being there for me that weekend.

At one point during that weekend, Judi, the kids and I went to Wal-mart. I'm sure I bought some pretty wild items that day because I have no recollection of what I paid for, only that I didn't say NO when the kids asked for things. They still talk about the fact that before this life changing event, I would buy them Pop Tarts, but only the ones without chocolate in them. The "healthier" ones, if you will. However, after the affair, I have bought them any Pop Tart flavor they desired. I, on the other hand, had lost seventeen pounds from Friday to Tuesday on that Labor Day weekend. This is not a weight loss program I would recommend.

7

My interactions with Brian were scattered throughout the weekend. I wanted to know where he was but I didn't want to look at him. I loved him and hated him all at the same time. For months afterward I would still say, "I love you, you jerk." Opposite emotions were constantly fighting for my attention. I would laugh when crying would be appropriate. I would scream my prayers sometimes. I remember asking God if everything Brian told me was a lie. Has he had multiple affairs? Did everyone on the planet know this except me? Was I an idiot? How could I not have seen this happening?

I don't think I was ever mad at God. I was so grateful that He was holding me together. I could feel His love for me, but I was so scared and frustrated because I didn't know what my future would look like. It was this strange world of feeling every emotion possible at the same time. Moving from one emotion to another without cause or warning. That first weekend especially, I felt like I had a small pool floaty and I was thrown into the deep ocean, just clinging to that little floaty for dear life praying that the waves would die down. I was frozen in situations that I would normally move through with ease and without a second thought. I remember picking out peanut butter for the kids a few weeks after the affair and I couldn't decide what brand and if I should get creamy or crunchy. I must have stood there staring at the peanut butter for five minutes and then feeling ridiculous because I couldn't decide. I went home that day with no peanut butter.

8

Before "D-Day," we had been studying an in-depth book in our small group called "One To One Discipling." It's the kind of book that forces Bible research and looking up numerous verses and questioning their meaning. This is my kind of book. Prior to this, one of the verses we were reading was Psalm 139: 5-6. Now, I had most likely read and/or heard this verse a thousand times in my life. I had probably memorized it in Awana Clubs! This time, these verses really resonated with me like my heart had just read them for the first time.

"You hem me in, behind and before,
and you lay your hand upon me.
 Such knowledge is too wonderful for me,
too lofty for me to attain."

Many of us are familiar with the passage leading up to these verses:
"You have searched me, LORD,
and you know me.
 You know when I sit and when I rise;
you perceive my thoughts from afar.
 You discern my going out and my lying down;
you are familiar with all my ways.

Before a word is on my tongue
you, LORD, know it completely."

I tried to go to bed that first night. I hadn't eaten since breakfast and the thought of food made me gag. Every time I closed my eyes my body would try to rest, but my mind was in overdrive. I was exhausted physically and emotionally, but when I would lay down and shut my eyes images would flood my mind. Images of him with someone else. I prayed and cried and prayed and cried. I walked around the house. I would check the boys in their bedrooms. Sidney was at a friend's house. I remember looking at the clock and it was 4:10 a.m. I was in my bedroom at the foot of the bed when God brought those beautiful words to my mind. It wasn't an audible voice, but it felt like God was speaking audibly to me:

"You hem me in, behind and before,
and you lay your hand upon me.
Such knowledge is too wonderful for me,
too lofty for me to attain."

I am not a seamstress. I can barely sew on the occasional button. However, I do know what a hem is. According to Dictionary.com the definition of "to hem in" is: to surround in a restrictive manner, to border, environ, surround, skirt or ring. To extend on all sides of simultaneously; encircle; to hedge, to hinder or restrict with or as if with a hedge. This definition especially resonated with me: to hem in first with stakes and nets so as to prevent them from going back into the sea with the ebb.

God was holding me in the palm of his hand. He was in front of me. He was behind me and when my life flipped upside down, he hemmed me in. He surrounded me. That incredible promise will amaze and humble me for the rest of my life. I was hemmed in. I didn't have the strength to hang on but I didn't have to because I was hemmed in. I was secure in my Father's hands.

God was hemming me in because He didn't want me to float around in the vast sea with no direction and to be subject to the ebb and flow of the world. I love this promise!

I don't think this made me sleep any better, but it certainly comforted me that night. God's word is alive. His word never changes, but can and will meet us where we are. His word will provide comfort, convict, direct and change our hearts. I have lived on those words in many dark moments since that day.

Many days while driving the kids to school, I would say, "Remember I love you and you are hemmed in." I know they got the point and it didn't take them long. A couple weeks afterwards, as we were driving into the school parking lot, I hadn't even said a word yet and one of them said, "We know, Mom. We know you love us and we are hemmed in…. We get it." Okay. I'm grateful they heard me and knew this truth. As much as it was something for them to hang onto during this time, it made it seem more real every time I said it out loud. It didn't make me stop saying it and praying it over them all the time.

9

I obviously learned so much from that first day, those first hours after finding out that Brian had been unfaithful. One of the many things I learned is that God's grace is never ending. It doesn't run dry. This illustration is not original to me, but it really encouraged me then and still does today. God's grace is sufficient for me EVERY DAY. It's like a magic pocket that always has enough money in it for you at that moment. Some days you might not even go to the store, but other days you are running errands all over town and spending a lot of money throughout the day. If I go through the drive thru at a restaurant and spend $6.00, I reach in my pocket and have exactly $6.00 to give. Then, I go to the grocery store and buy $200 worth of food for my hungry family... I reach into that previously empty pocket and I have exactly $200 to pay for my groceries. Then, I stop at the gas station... you get the idea.

This is how God's grace is. I might have a crazy day with mad, unsatisfied customers and then get in an accident on the way home from work. I then could have my kids mad at me for forgetting to pay for their school lunches that month and now it's too late. Once I'm home, I burn dinner and have to order a pizza, which is honestly what my family wanted in the first place. God's grace is full and complete to get me through this day. The day I found out about Brian's affair, God's grace got me through that day… and frankly got Brian through that day. God's grace was sufficient even for Brian in that day and every day.

Seriously, when we have a day where things are going great, God's grace is sufficient for that day as well. God doesn't give us an equal amount of His grace each day and when we run out… well we run out. NO. He gives us an endless supply of His grace and power as we need it. I know God allows us to go through trials in our daily lives to draw us closer to Him. He wants us to lean on HIM, be led by HIM and give HIM the glory.

10

My sister and I were on the way to run an errand with the kids that first crazy weekend when we passed by one of our neighbors in his yard. He happened to be a director in the department I worked in at my place of employment. He was coincidentally a good friend of Brian's and (an irony not lost) they were also accountability partners. He was in his front yard with his wife, when I told my sister to pull over so I could talk to him. I asked him if I could change my hours for a couple weeks so I could drop the kids off at school each day. His wife saw me and couldn't find words. We were not close friends, but I saw the pain on her face. People truly did not know what to say or how to help. I certainly didn't know what I needed at that time, except for prayer. I know the prayers of many people were graciously answered by our loving God.

I went back to work on Tuesday after Labor Day. I couldn't concentrate. I am sure I looked out of my mind because I was. I sat there taking the first call and tried my best to hold it together. When the second call came, things suddenly took on a new light.

The call was from a pushy agent who told me in a very demanding tone what he needed and that he needed it now. Oftentimes, you would have an agent call and right out of the gate tell you that he's been in the business for 20 years and he's a successful, extremely busy person who doesn't have time to answer your silly questions. We are required to verify the caller to make sure they are who they say they are, and that they have access to the information in the referenced account. Out of habit, I asked the basic questions that we are required to ask at the beginning of each phone call to verify the caller. He impatiently answered my questions, but finally said, "Look, you need to hurry up."

I calmly said, "Can I have your name, please?"
He said, "Brian."

Well, no other name on the planet could evoke the passionate response I had for this caller. I cannot remember the exact words, but it was something like, "Ok. Listen, *Brian*. I will get you the information you need, but first *you* need to realize that being pushy will not get you anywhere with me. I would appreciate it if you would change your tone. You are no more important than any other caller I talk to on any other day. I have no problem getting the information you requested, but we are going to do this my way. I need to put you on hold for a moment while I get your information." When I got back on the line "Brian" was the nicest, most appreciative patient caller I'd ever had. He was overly apologetic and thanked me for my time profusely. I had really let him have it. He had no idea the different response he would have gotten if his

35

name were "Paul." And the response from my co-workers that heard that phone call was priceless. I think they were even a little scared of me.

11

Brian said several times during that first weekend that he was glad I could go back to work to get my mind off this mess. I've learned that men can compartmentalize, which I believe is partly how he got himself *into* this mess. Most women do not compartmentalize very well. Every cell in my body had been affected that day. Every thought changed. The way I viewed the world changed.

I used to walk down the street or the hallway at work and see people and think, "Oh my gosh, she is cute. I bet she's fun. I love that necklace!" Or "cute shoes!" Now I see people and think, "I bet he cheats on his wife" and "I bet she's a liar." I miss the way I used to view people. Maybe it was naïve but it's a world I still miss.

Every cell in my body changed when he spoke those words, "The accusations are true." Every outlook I had was altered. I looked through different eyes. My counselor said that I had more clarity about everything in my view than ever before in my life. I was bolder about my decisions. I was more decisive when facing big decisions.

The kids really struggled with the aftermath of the news of Brian's infidelity. Generally, you wouldn't tell your kids in a situation like ours. Brian was a well-known preacher in the area, and the communities we were involved in overlapped. We knew the kids had to know because we didn't want them to hear inadvertently.

Sidney and her father have had a rocky relationship and they hate it when I say this, but they are a lot like. Their outlook and response to life is very similar. Brian doesn't have much gray area in his life. It's black and white and Sidney is even more so. It's taken a long time for them to work through this together. Brian demands respect because he's her father and Sidney believes he should earn that respect back. Keaton and Trenton both did not want to talk about it. They both had moments when they would cry or be in their thoughts, but getting back into the routine of school after that awful weekend was a good relief for them. Mostly, everyone was respectful of the kids' privacy and simply loved them through this.

On the other hand, I became the newly elected poster child for faithful wife of the cheating husband. I cannot begin to tell you the number of people that approached me saying, "Nobody knows this, but my husband cheated on me and we're working on saving our marriage…" Working to save your marriage is huge, don't get me wrong. I'm glad people feel they can talk to me about this struggle, and if I can be a listening ear or give sound advice then hopefully I'm bringing glory to God through this mess. But, working on your marriage after an affair is hard work. Working on your marriage after an affair that was pretty public in our community is super hard. I did have sort of a sick sense of security that it wouldn't happen again because there were so many eyes watching him.

Often, I'll have a friend or acquaintance say that they have a friend that is working through a similar situation and could they meet with me. I will never say no to this. It is a way to reach outside of myself and my own pain to listen and share in someone else's life. Yes, they are usually emotional talks and it always brings me back to my pain, but there is also so much healing in these conversations for me.

I am not alone. Many of these people have no hope or are running really low on hope. Even if their relationship doesn't stay together, there is always hope that God will provide and heal and grow you out of these terrible experiences. I also never want these people to think that they are alone. If we can share, cry, laugh, pray together and bring some hope and clarity to a situation, then the tragedy in my own life was not in vain. This is one way to bring glory to God in strengthening marriages. If talking to me because I've been there brings a sense of not being alone to someone, I'm all for it. Use me, Lord.

12

When Pastor Jim first started working through all of this with us he asked me what I wanted. I told him that if Brian was remorseful I would work to forgive him. I told him that I didn't want to give Satan another Christian marriage.

Through all the weeds, I was put in contact with a strong Christian woman who had faced a similar crisis in her marriage, and it was also very public. We met for breakfast one day and she encouraged me to continue to be faithful and move forward in my healing. I knew her family casually and after hearing her story realized that I knew the "other woman" in her situation. I had never spoken with this "other woman" but I knew who she was from church and the kids' school. About nine months after our public mess, I was at a school event with my kids.

We have an annual fund raiser called Jog-a-thon and the students raise pledges from family and friends. They run laps around a course and people will give a flat donation or a certain dollar amount per lap. Trenton had just run 28 laps, which is huge, and then he ate not one, but two walking tacos. They were not just walking around his stomach -- they were also doing laps. He was not feeling great and I needed to get him home. Well, as we were making our way through the crowds, this "other woman" approached me in this crowded gym with Trenton right next to me. She said that she was sorry about what I had gone through, but if I ever wanted to hear about it from another perspective to let her know and she would gladly sit down with me. WHAT??!!?? I quickly said, "Thank you, but I have no need for that perspective, this one is hard enough," and I walked away with Trenton as a witness to it all.

13

I know people didn't know what to do to help us. *I* didn't know what to do. Right as the rumor mill began, I started to get texts and phone calls from close friends and not so close friends. Some texted and wanted details. "Did you catch them in the act? Do you know her? How long was the affair?" I didn't respond to most of these questions.

I had people call or text to say they were praying and that they were available if I needed anything. I really and truly appreciated all the prayers. It's what carried me through. This is why our marriage survived. People prayed. We worked, and people prayed.

Pastor Jim was supposed to be out of town that Labor Day weekend and Brian was supposed to preach. Pastor Jim called me and told me that he was staying in town and would be preaching on forgiveness. He said, "This sermon is not for you. You have a long journey to travel towards forgiveness." The sermon he preached was about forgiving each other in the body of Christ.

After the service, the church leaders asked the church body to stay for a short meeting. During this meeting, the church body was told that Brian Clay had a "moral failing," and would no longer be on staff at Brookside Church. This was not expounded on but people filled in the blanks.

I certainly did not attend that Sunday's church service, so anyone who had not heard on Friday or Saturday through the grapevine knew about our situation after that day.

During the following week, a letter was sent out from the church leaders to all of the church body to let everyone know that Brian Clay had a "moral failing" and would not be on staff at Brookside Church anymore. It asked that everyone be praying for Brian and his family during this time. It also let the reader know that the ministries of the church remained strong and vibrant.

Our church leaders wanted to let the congregation know that Brookside Church remained strong. They wanted Brian and our family to be prayed for and loved, but this letter created a whole new wave of awareness to people who had missed church on Labor Day weekend. It also reached to people who hadn't attended Brookside in months.

I know that the letter's intent was not to hurt us as a family. Perhaps a couple of the reasons for the letter was to quiet the questions as to why Brian was not on staff anymore at the church and to dispel any rumors that followed. Again, I know that many people were praying for our family when this happened and these prayers to our Holy God got me through. I felt comforted, loved and cared for, while simultaneously, feeling like I was in a fish bowl being watched intently by many people.

The kids wanted to go to church the next week, so I took them. They went to their Sunday School classes and I sat alone in the church service. It was treacherous. Even though I know people in that church love my family and me, I felt very exposed. People cried. People hugged. Some people avoided me. People stared. I sat towards the back so I could sneak in and out if I needed to. One family walked in and scooted into a row about eight rows in front of me. The mother in the family saw me and whispered to her husband. He turned around and looked at me. Then a few minutes later, another couple came in and sat next to them. The woman leaned over to her new pew mate and whispered to her with a flick of her thumb pointing back at me. So, of course, this woman tells her husband and he has a look, too.

I know somewhere deep in my heart that they were not being malicious. I had a wonderful counselor tell me that these people were in awe of me. They were not judging me. They knew in their hearts they couldn't do what I was doing by forgiving my husband. I felt very vulnerable and ostracized because people didn't know what to do with me.

About two weeks after finding out about Brian's affair, I asked his office manager to meet for breakfast one Saturday. She is the only woman I know that can keep one step ahead of Brian regarding his schedule. Now, I did believe that she didn't know about the affair and didn't condone it or cover it up, but I still needed to look her in the eyes and have that conversation. From the lashing she gave Brian when it all hit the fan, I knew she was hurt by his deception as well. We met and talked and cried and it gave me peace.

You must understand that when a deep deception like this happens, you really don't know what the facts are anymore. Was this just one of many affairs? Was I the only one who didn't know about his cheating? Was I a fool? A laughing stock? Paranoia can set in and do crazy things to your mind if you let it.

Many visits with my counselor and long talks with good friends helped me stay focused. I found myself constantly going to prayer saying, "Lord, please remove this doubt. Help me to trust. Lord, please give me direction. Help me to see clearly." I would breathe prayers going into the grocery store or into the kids' school. It's the way we, as Christians, should live every day, but during this time it was much more of a constant necessity for me.

Praise God, I knew a few things that were true. God's love for me was real. I was hemmed in, remember? I was standing on solid ground. Very few things made sense, but I knew who I was with

God and that was more than enough to get me through each long painful day. **"Because of the LORD's great love we are not consumed, for his compassions never fail. They are new every morning; great is your faithfulness."** Lamentation 3:22-23

I know that I am a child of the one true God. I am royalty. I am an heir to the throne. Romans 5:1-5 says, **"Therefore, since we have been justified by faith, we have peace with God through our Lord Jesus Christ. Through Him we have also obtained access by faith into this grace in which we stand, and we rejoice in hope of the glory of God. Not only that, but we rejoice in our sufferings, knowing that suffering produces endurance, and endurance produces character, and character produces hope, and hope does not put us to shame, because God's love has been poured into our hearts through the Holy Spirit who has been given to us."**

Now, please realize I was not and am not rejoicing in this suffering. BUT, because of this situation I am stronger in my faith, stronger in my relationships, and able to share with other people the hope that I have in Jesus Christ. Would I want this to happen if I could go back? NO! But since it did I can rejoice in the fact that God has grown me through this situation to be closer to Him. I am a child of God. I am loved. I am strengthened through this. That is what I rejoice in.

I John 3:1 says how much God loves us. We are His children. **"See what great love the Father has lavished on us, that we should be called children of God! And that is what we are! The reason the world does not know us is that it did not know him."**

14

About six months after "D-Day," I was leaving Target by myself and I saw a man and a woman standing by a running car in the parking lot. They were talking and kissing and laughing. I sat and watched them for a few minutes and knew that they were cheating in some way. Neither one had a target uniform on so it wasn't like one of them was on break and the spouse was bringing dinner or whatever. If they were together they could get in the car and drive home. If they were supposed to be together, why were they hanging out in a cold parking lot?

My gut told me they were cheating. My wounded heart told me they were bound to hurt someone else by this parking lot meeting. I wanted to scream at them across the parking lot, which probably would have been comical in some way. I drove away, but I still believe my heart was in tune with that deception. My counselor told me I probably was right about that situation and that maybe I should have said something to possibly derail a situation that had the potential to hurt a lot of people. I do believe she was right and looking back, I should have said something. I could have saved some hurt for the families being affected by whatever, if anything, was going on.

I remember about a week after finding out about the affair having lunch at work with a bunch of people I didn't know very well. I was sitting with my friend, when a few people just came and sat down with us, which is usually fine, but my friend was trying to encourage me and it was a rather private conversation. I cherished those private moments whenever I could get them because there didn't seem to be much privacy in my life at this point.

Well, this rather nosey lady jumped right into our conversation and assumed correctly that I had been cheated on. She leaned across the table towards me, pointed her manicured finger at me and said, "Take it from one who knows, get out while you can. Once a cheater, always a cheater." Well, thank you for your uninvited input person I've never met before! I was blown away by her directness, but I believe in her own scary way she was saying to me what many people who were closer to the situation didn't want to say to me. I could understand her directness and boldness because I adopted much of my own since that first day. She obviously had first-hand experience with this and she was warning me to be aware and to remain strong.

Several women over the last few years have approached me to share their marital struggles with me. Many have said that they and their husbands have grown apart or "they fell out of love with each other."

Yes. I know my marital struggles have been public here in our little realm, but I would boldly tell these women to hang on and work hard for their marriages. Yes, I know marriage is hard. God will reward your faithfulness. He will make beauty out of ashes. I chose to stay. And sometimes I have to make that decision intentionally every day. I recommend you pray for a long time before you decide to leave your spouse. Yes. I believe that God leads us all differently, but His Word is His Word and He despises divorce.

Do not stay in an abusive relationship. You have every right to leave if your spouse has an affair. But love is a decision, not a feeling. We are commanded to love in the Bible. God tells us in Matthew 5:44, **"But I say to you, love your enemies and pray for those who persecute you."** Loving others is not easy all the time. Jesus specifically says, Love your enemies because it's hard work and it's a conscious decision. You have to deliberately choose to love. He doesn't say "love your best friend and your family" because that's easy. He is saying loving others is hard.

Now, don't get me wrong. Your spouse is not your enemy, they can be very unlovable sometimes, but so can each of us. If you choose to divorce, please go to God about it first. This decision will affect more than just you. I am not saying that God cannot use you if you choose to divorce. He can and will use all of us if we let Him. God is so much bigger than our situations. He sees the big picture. We do not.

I loved what Brian and I had. I love what we have today. We have a wonderful family. He makes me crazy but I love him so much. He still is the funniest person I know. I can't imagine living life with anyone else.

15

He tells us in Micah 6:8, **"He has told you, O man, what is good; and what does the Lord require of you but to do justice, and to love kindness, and to walk humbly with your God."** I believe we need to take ownership of our sin and our garbage and grow from our mistakes. If we strive to serve God in our actions and outlooks, He will grow us as individuals and heal any mess we have made. God is the Almighty Healer. He can and will heal our hurts and our relationships, but both parties need to be open and willing. He gives us guidelines, but He also gives us grace. And, most of all, Brian was willing to heal our marriage. This is most often not the case. You cannot, obviously, save a marriage by yourself.

I will not judge because I was judged in the weakest, most vulnerable time of my life and it was no picnic in the park. I also will not sugar coat it. If you approach me I will listen. I will pray with you. I will do my best to encourage you. If you tell me that you and your spouse have grown apart and you are still friends, but are going to divorce, I will say that is NOT God's will for your life. That is not how God intended your marriage to be. It says so in His Word.

It says in Matthew 19: 5-6, **"For this reason a man will leave his father and mother and be united to his wife, and the two will become one flesh. So they are no longer two, but one flesh. Therefore, what God has joined together, let man not separate."** Marriage is hard work, but trust me when I say if you are both faithful to God and each other and truly work at it, God will honor this and bless your marriage. Again, God can and will use you individually, but He could have done great things through you as a married couple as well.

16

I never thought adultery would touch my life. Maybe I lived in a bubble. I know I was naïve regarding many things in the world and I thank God for protecting me from many evils of the world for so many years. I view the world differently now than I did before. I don't let people get close to me very often anymore. I love befriending people, but it's different than it was. I, unfortunately, don't give my all to everyone anymore, and it's unfortunate because that innocent trusting is gone.

Believing that every new person I meet will view me with fresh eyes and promise, like I viewed them, is also gone. I had many friends and acquaintances that I liked and trusted. That is no longer the case. I have this sickness that I want everyone to like me. I've always wanted this since I can remember. I loved to make people laugh. I wanted to see people smile. As cliché as it sounds, I wanted to make the world a better place by spreading a little joy. Well, fast-forward after this time in my life, and my viewpoint has definitely changed.

My outlook of the world has changed just in the way I view people. Our world is full of broken people. My prayer life has been ignited with a burden for people who need God in their lives and hearts AND their marriages.

I started hating crowds because I didn't know where this woman was and what she knew about me. I didn't know who knew what or what they thought they knew. I didn't trust anyone. This one act changed my relationship with Brian of course. It changed my relationship with my family and his family. It changed my relationships with friends. I began to carefully select who I allowed to get close to me, those who would be kept at a distance, and those who were not friends at all. It changed my relationship with God and my dependence on Him. I am still trusting, seeing the best in people, but I am not as quick to do so anymore.

17

Brian and I were part of a small group for over a decade when this happened. We had such a great support system in these people and they truly felt like family to us. They were there for me the night it all went down. They even brought me sleeping medicine when I couldn't rest. They showed us such amazing support. Brian and I couldn't have gotten through what we did without the strength of these dear people in our lives.

After a while though, I really struggled meeting with them. It was a number of things. It was literally a "it's me not you" issue. I felt as if they wanted me to move on, get over it and make it all happy, happy again. This group had allowed me to share my heart, my struggles, and my hurts up until this time. Now, I was "expected" to be all better, and back to normal, but I couldn't do that, at least not at their pace. This was unchartered water.

At one point, one of my friends from the group took me out to dinner and told me that I needed to quit being worried about the people at church and their stares. These were the feelings I would share with my small group because I felt I could. I wasn't sharing these things with everyone I met on the street. But I felt that I could share honestly, because I was emotionally in the healing process and what I was going through with my small group since they had been there from the beginning.

I was told that night at dinner that I would have to realize that people in the church have "moved on" to the next bit of gossip or whatever. It had been six months. I needed to move on and realize that most people didn't care anymore; it was old news. I know she was well meaning. I know she wanted to help me grow from this point and realize things were going to be okay, and she loved me. This was not where I was.

I was dealing with a lot of emotions and pain every day and this didn't help. It mostly made me realize I couldn't share my heart anymore with my small group. They had helped me immensely and then didn't have the capacity to after a while. For me, my small group wasn't a safe place anymore.

Brian had started teaching again in our small group and it was just "like old times." I couldn't handle it. It was too soon for me. I didn't need a place to bash Brian or cry the ugly cry at every small group meeting, I just needed the freedom to do so if I needed to. Sometimes I felt selfish leaving the group, but it was time to truly move on. I needed to be free to heal at my own pace. I still love these people to this day. They were rocks for me and for Brian when we needed them the most. I'm forever grateful to all of them.

18

When all of this happened, we had a cleaning lady coming twice a month to help us keep up with the house since Brian and I were both working full time. I loved cleaning days because it was such a relief to come home and have a clean house, even if it only lasted for (what seemed like) a few minutes. Afterwards, it bothered me to have someone in the house when we weren't home.

My home, my safe place had been violated and I didn't want anyone in my house without being there myself. I let the cleaning lady go that first week after the affair. I hated the thought of what had happened in my home without my knowledge. Like the violation of our wedding vows wasn't enough, the simultaneous violation of our home was just too much for me to stomach.

The friend who cleaned for us probably didn't understand the change because she was suddenly out of a cleaning job, but it had to happen. I was much bolder about what I needed and wanted than I had ever been, so I think I shocked a lot of people by stating my opinion without apologies. This was a sudden change in me. Something ignited inside of me. Many people were asking me how I was feeling and how I was doing. I knew they wanted the truth and I would tell them. Now, I wasn't getting into huge weep sessions with people I didn't know very well, but I could say, "it's a tough day today" or, "every day seems to get a bit easier." I wouldn't just say, "Fine, thank you." Because I wasn't.

I think I was instantly vulnerable when people heard the news and I didn't have the strength to build up any walls. Again, I wasn't a blubbering ugly crier (in public anyway), but I was living at a deeper level emotionally and still do to this day.

The affair made me more introspective. I could share my heart or my state of mind and not feel I had to defend my feelings. I could share "this is how I feel today, this is what I'm struggling with in this process right now" and not feel I had to explain it all to make the listener feel good about it. I didn't have to resolve it for anyone else because in most cases I hadn't resolved it for myself yet. I had always wanted to make people smile or laugh in any interaction with me. Seriously, often to my family's dismay, I will make friends with the drive thru worker. But if people I worked with or people at church would say, "How are you?" I allowed myself to say, "It's rough right now, please pray for me." Before the affair, I may have been struggling, but I wouldn't share my needs as easily with other people. I would say, "Oh, I'm fine," and have a quick surface conversation. I think I believed people didn't really want to know the truth, so I would brush my own needs off and not share them or ask for help. But when this happened, I was vulnerable and most people at the school and the church knew the situation, so when they asked me, I would share a little, and I saw their sincerity too. Most people sincerely cared and I allowed myself to be open to them.

With that being said, I pulled away from a lot of casual friends and some close friends. I couldn't be everyone's friend anymore. I loved people, but I realized I had the power to choose my close friends so I did just that. God was setting up a solid group of friends for me even before news of the affair had become common knowledge. It's amazing when I think about it, but I had three dear friends that were not all friends with each other, but I asked them all to breakfast one day about a year before the affair. We talked and talked and talked and they listened to me. We prayed together, we cried, but mostly we laughed. These three women have been a Godsend. They have let me be me. They let me take my time when I need to. They let me hurry up when I need to. They have comforted me. I even threw up on one of them. These are true blue friends. They even think I'm funny sometimes! More than just inviting them to breakfast that one day long ago, God has bound us together. He truly has blessed our friendship. Many days and many breakfasts have seen awful tragedies in all of our lives, but it has been a privilege and an honor to walk through life being friends with these amazing, Godly, hysterically funny women.

19

One month after D-day, one of these dear friends faced a very similar situation in her marriage, but it involved her husband and a longtime friend. Well, she was actually a witness to an awkward situation with the two of them. She, in fact, punched the awful friend in the face. I don't know what I would have done in that situation, but when relaying this happening to Brian, he said, "Would you have done that if you walked in on us?" I quickly said, "No, I'm more of a hair-puller." I thought that was a hilarious response. Brian, not so much.

My friend had a long battle to save her marriage and as awful a mess as she was dealing with I was grateful to have someone next to me to walk through the weeds. She had lost a friend as well. There was so much pent up hurt and anger, but she and her husband continually gave it to God and He took them and molded their hearts and healed their wounds. He is still doing an amazing work in their lives and the lives of their family. God is at work if only we let Him.

I wish there was a way to let people know where you are emotionally on a broad scale when faced with something like this. And there is: if you know someone is hurting, pray for them. If you sense someone is struggling, pray for them. God knows the facts - you don't need to. Stop and ask if you can pray with them. Please know that people going through tough times need to talk about it, but they also get to choose who they share the facts with (for the most part.) If someone doesn't answer your questions... yep, you guessed it! Pray for them!

In those first few days, I was overwhelmed with texts and calls from everyone and their brother. Many people wanted to let me know they were praying for me, which is exactly what I needed. Others, however, were trying to get the scoop or trying to be in that inner circle. Many asked, "Who was it?" "Do you know her?" "Did you catch them in the act?" "Where did they do it?" "How long has it been going on?" Seriously, people? If you ever find yourself in a similar situation, my prayer is that people won't bombard you with questions like these. It was very easy to mark many friends off my great friends list after getting texts and phone calls like these.

Then there were the few who called and said, "Can I come and sit with you?" Well, I might not have taken this the right way, but it seemed like they wanted to conduct a counseling session in my living room or to get the juicy facts. I will invite you if I want you here. Thanks. I had one good friend text and say she wanted to come pray with me. Normally I would say "of course," but I wasn't ready for company. I wasn't ready. I told her no, I am not sure what shape I'll be in. She responded, "I'll take you in any shape," I said,

"No, please just pray for me from where you are." She understood, but it was difficult for me to stand up for myself and my privacy (what was left of it), but I felt empowered once I started setting those boundaries.

20

About six months after the affair Brian and I decided to have my wedding ring redone. When my mom passed away in 2008, I received her diamond from my dad. It is pear shaped and when Brian was looking for rings for me, I told him that I'd love any ring from him, but it would be super special if it was pear shaped like my mom's. So, I have a beautiful pear shaped diamond ring like my mom's.

After this turmoil, we took the rings to a jeweler and they designed this gorgeous one-of-a-kind ring. While the ring was being made, which took about a month, my ring finger was naked. Can you just imagine the firestorm this created? I'm not upset with people for noticing or with people wondering or being concerned, but with all the questions I was originally asked (and people asked some really intrusive questions…) none of these "wondering and concerned" people came directly to me. Several people approached close friends of mine asking, "Is Jill ok? She's not wearing a ring." "I saw Jill at church and noticed her ring isn't on? Are Brian and Jill ok?" I get that people are concerned, but PLEASE don't gossip or guess or pass judgement. PLEASE just stop what you are doing and PRAY! God knows the situation from the inside out. PLEASE just pray for that person or that situation. The details are none of your business. I went to the store and bought a cheap little (turn my finger green) band in the interim, but honestly, I beg of you DON'T TALK TO ANYONE ABOUT WHAT YOU SEE OR DON'T SEE. IT JUST CREATES HURT. JUST PRAY.

I have come to realize that people didn't really know me, and that they would automatically assume that what they thought they would do in a similar situation is exactly what I should do or would do. These people were wrong. God was at work. I understand people's first reaction is to flee. Please understand, that would have been my gut reaction sitting with a friend who was facing this. People, you don't know how you will react until you are in the situation yourself. My own reactions surprised me, so trust me when I say you have no idea how you will respond if in a similar situation. I'm so grateful God took over because I was so weak and numb. My responses were His responses and that was my prayer. The decision to stay is not everyone's decision. This is not the answer in every marriage. I do not judge the decisions of others, please understand that. I am simply telling you what God led me to do in our marriage.

Years before I had a friend facing a really rough patch in her marriage, so I prayed for her and tried to be there for her when she needed to talk. I had given her the verse, Exodus 14:14, "**The LORD will fight for you; you need only to be still.**" This verse follows the verses where the Israelites have fled Egypt and Pharaoh had sent 600 chariots and warriors out to chase them down and kill them. The Israelites were asking Moses, "Why did we leave Egypt to die out in the desert? What was the point of this?" Moses told them, "The Lord will fight for you; you need only to be still." In the next few verses God parts the Red Sea. His miracle was coming; they just needed to trust Him.

When my friend was facing this, she didn't know what to do. She was trying to figure out how to solve this. This verse really spoke volumes in her situation. God was working, she needed to be still and let God work.

Years later when I was facing turmoil she sent this verse to me. I love how God's Word is alive. His Word meets the needs of people in every generation, in every language, in every situation. God's word is such a gift to us.

I had such peace remembering and holding on to the promise of this verse. The Lord will fight for me. I wasn't alone. I didn't know what tomorrow would look like. I didn't know what five minutes from now would look like, but the God of the universe, my God, was fighting for me. What an amazing, personal, overwhelming promise. I was "hemmed" in. I was safe in His mighty hands.

21

I know Brian wanted to reconcile our marriage and his relationship with the church. We had our work cut out for us. We took many months and concentrated on our family as well as us as a couple. We went to counseling together, as well as separately and I really grew a lot. I had always disliked self-help, do it yourself, grow your prayer life type books simply because they seem so common sense-ish.

When this happened in my life, my counselor recommended a book to me entitled: <u>Torn Asunder: Recovering From An Extra-Marital Affair</u>, by Dave Carder. This book was so essential in helping me put the pieces back together. Nothing in my life was "common-sense-ish" anymore and I read this book over and over. I ate the book whole. At the counseling session a week later I told her I had read the whole book. I think she thought I would take my time, but I needed some sort of guidance and direction to start on this journey and this amazing book set the ground work for me.

Towards the end of the book, however, there was a chapter that really bothered me. It talked about how after working through the beginning of the healing process, you should find another couple to come along side you. This couple should be people that you both feel comfortable with sharing what happened in your marriage. You are to share about your healing process and ask for encouragement and prayer support.

Well, this really ticked me off. The option of telling people when I felt I was ready had been robbed from me. The world around me in Fort Wayne, Indiana already knew! It bothered me because I wasn't given the option of telling people myself. In a situation like ours it was difficult because I didn't know who knew what. Many people thought they knew the situation. Also, to add another layer, I knew the other woman's name but had never met her. What was she telling people? Who was she telling? I was hiding and dodging like a criminal trying to stay away from nosy people.

I was healing in public. I wasn't given the choice. There were times when I would drop the kids off at church on Sunday morning and then instead of going to the service, go get an iced tea or go to the grocery store and then be there to pick them up when church was over. I couldn't handle the feeling of being watched. Although, I knew through all of this that no one was judging me, it was still a strange feeling to have people watch me. I knew people, in the majority, were praying for me and wishing me well.

I started having panic attacks. There was one time at Kroger that my cart was full of groceries and I was heading down the last aisle. I do not know what triggered it except that I was weirded out by people watching me or the idea that people were watching me. Now, I realize that no one is going out of their way to watch me, especially at Kroger, but my mind was doing crazy things at this time. I walked away from that full cart and left the store. I sat in my car in the parking lot for about 15 minutes and tried to catch my breath. Then, I went back in the store, found my cart, acted like I knew what I was doing, purchased my cart full of groceries and went home.

Sidney, Von, my mother in law, and I were Christmas shopping a couple of months after the affair, and I started to feel like people were watching me, knowing me or stuff about me… and not knowing this woman… she could be standing right next to me. My mind started swimming in that crowded mall. I tried to talk myself down, but within ten minutes, I was getting sick in the bathroom. I hated this. How is it that my husband is seemingly moving on with his life all right?

I don't know this woman, but if she can do the things she did, she's probably not getting sick in the mall bathroom after a panic attack or losing sleep over this mess. I know that God is working on them both. I just have to trust and worry about how God is growing me. Brian and this other woman should be the one's getting sick at the mall and losing sleep night after night.

For a while, Brian would tell people to leave me alone. To quit asking me questions. To realize that I had nothing to do with this sin in his life, it was him not me who was deficient in our marriage. My counselor said the following: "I believe it would be easier for him to feel like he is defending your honor than to expose his own sin." This made so much sense to me. He was spending energy fighting for my honor rather than the introspective hard work of figuring out what allowed him to commit adultery. I know that Brian's counselor was trying to get to the core of his sin, and in those months of counseling he was challenged, and he worked hard.

Counseling was a lifesaver for me, although it was difficult each and every time. It was like nothing I'd ever experienced. Sharing my heart with someone was refreshing, but also emotionally draining. Learning to forgive, truly forgive. How to start to trust again? How not to hold onto bitterness? How to show my children how to embrace forgiveness and move toward healing all while trying to do it myself?

I remember driving across town to my sessions just knowing I was going into a danger zone of emotions, and then, when I'd drive home, I'd turn the radio off and just zone. You know that feeling when you get to an intersection and not remember how you got there? It was exhausting.

22

When you choose to be authentic and honorable and strive to grow in Christ, you will be open with those closest to you about the choices you are making. At the point in Brian's life when he fell, he was compartmentalizing the different areas of his life. Brian could function, or so he told himself, in work mode, home mode and church mode without allowing the one part to infiltrate the others. He chose to find this woman and commit this sin. He could then go and function in the other areas of his life (apparently) like normal.

When Brian went through counseling services he had to confront this aspect of his life. How he could make wise decisions and smart moves in his life, and then at literally the same time be making unethical and immoral decisions. It brings a group of verses to mind whenever I think of this: Jeremiah 17:7- 10,

"Blessed is the man who trusts in the Lord,
whose trust is the Lord.
He is like a tree planted by water,
that sends out its roots by the stream,
and does not fear when heat comes,
for its leaves remain green,
and is not anxious in the year of drought,
for it does not cease to bear fruit.

**The heart is deceitful above all things,
and desperately sick;
who can understand it?
I the Lord search the heart
and test the mind
to give every man according to his ways,
according to the fruit of his deeds."**

Verse 9 says the heart is deceitful above all things and desperately sick; who can understand it?

Often times, I'll be driving down the street listening to Christian music, singing along if no one else is in the car… and someone will cut me off or do something stupid and immediately my response will be nasty. I say something hateful, or at least think it. Now, I want my first response to be Christ like in all situations, but the heart is deceitful. I continue to work on this, but this girl has some road rage in her. I'm shocked that my first response is so ugly sometimes.

The heart is deceptive. This is why we must hide away the truths of the Bible in our hearts. The whole Garbage In = Garbage Out thing. If we put garbage into our minds and hearts that is what will eventually come out. It is so important to study God's word and be in prayer, but we truly never know how we will respond when tragedy strikes.

Brian's counselor told him that I would handle situations in public two drastically different ways, and he was absolutely right. When people approached us and treated Brian with love because they wanted him to know that he was forgiven, my internal response would be, "Are you kidding me? Do you have any idea what he did to me and my family?" Or if people treated him with disdain I would internally respond, "Are you serious right now? If I can forgive him, who the heck, are you?"

This was true on so many occasions. There was a man at church who, wanting Brian to know how loved and forgiven he was, literally stepped on my foot to get to Brian to hug him and tell him so. He did this for two weeks in a row. I'm so glad Brian is loved and forgiven, but I still guard my feet to this day when I see this man coming towards us.

23

Brian was loved by many people. Pastor Jim was one of his best friends. They spent many hours on Fridays and Saturdays together planning sermons and slides to go with them. They studied together and laughed together… mostly laughed together, I'm sure. They respected and loved each other so much. They would bounce ideas off one another and they both had a desire to grow the people in and around Brookside Church closer to God.

When Brian made this choice he devastated many people. Pastor Jim definitely was one of them, but he had to step up and keep the ministry going and at the same time try to help our marriage heal.

It would have been easier to walk away. I had every right to walk away. Biblically, I could divorce him. I know God hates divorce. I never felt that I HAD to stay in my marriage. I wanted to. I knew it was what God wanted me to do. I know many people who have divorced for less than adultery, and I do not judge their decision. That is seriously between them and God. But, God led me to stay, and as hard as it was and sometimes still is, I stayed.

Brian's reconciliation with the church was multifaceted. He was required to go to counseling alone and then with me. Brian was held accountable by attending meetings with our denomination President, Rocky Rocholl, on a weekly basis. He met before the denomination's board as well as the church board several times throughout the first two years. He also had an accountability group of two other men that held him accountable. Although I was pretty much over the accountability group idea since he was meeting with them when this whole thing started in the first place, he did continue to meet with these men and now they are truly great friends with Brian, and for that I am thankful. It just proves you can keep secrets from anyone.

At one counseling session, I said how mad I was that Brian had changed how our kids will view marriage and relationships forever. My counselor said, "Yes, he changed that, but now you are showing them what healthy healing is and most children never have that played out in front of them. You are giving them a gift."

When we met with the Elder Board a couple months after the affair, under the advisement of his counselor, Brian read an apology letter to them. Afterward, he shared with them the progress he was making in counseling. We then both answered questions from the Elders. It was a tough, emotional night, but the forgiveness already evident in that board room is something I will never forget. Those men then prayed for us. I don't think there was a dry eye in the room. These men showed such compassion for Brian and me. It was truly beautiful. Once this happened, I wanted our whole church to experience this full circle of repentance and forgiveness. **"We all have sinned and fallen short of the glory of God,"** says Romans 3:23. Of course, we are all sinners. Not one of us is without sin. We are striving to be Christ-like. We are all broken and in need of a Savior. Romans 6:23 says, **"The wages of sin is death, but the gift of God is eternal life through Jesus Christ our Lord."** Jesus paid the price for us to have a relationship with God. He paved the way for us to have eternal life with Him.

I believe that during the first meeting with the church board when Brian read his apology letter where we prayed and cried with these men, this should have spilled over to the whole congregation at that time. We had that moment two and half years later in front of the church, but I still believe that process could have been so powerful when our situation was still so fresh in the minds of so many people. Again, God's timing is perfect and he made it perfect in His time, but seeing that the healing and restoration process displayed for the church body could really have made a huge impact.

24

I believe that because of how public the announcement of Brian's failure was there needed to be closure and a chance for healing on the other side of this for everyone. Brian and I made it our goal to bring this restoration full circle for the people around us. Both of us wanted to have closure for the church body as well. Can you imagine the healing that would take place if this wasn't just locked away in a board room tidy and neat and not talked about? Can you imagine if our church could see the full circle, the hard work, the healing and be a part of it? It would take a lot of vulnerability on my part, but wasn't I already out there? People already knew. Why couldn't we allow God to continue the story in the eyes of the people around us?

It was actually Brian's birthday the day we met with the Elder Board, just for a little irony. What do you get a guy for his birthday a month and a half after he cheats on you? Well, God gave me a great idea. Really! Early in our marriage I worked with a girl who was engaged, and when the wedding came around she invited us. It was a beautiful gesture because I was so new to the office. It was a gorgeous wedding. We were in the sanctuary and the ceremony was the focus of the wedding, the reception was not. I respect that. The wedding party was huge. Literally, it took 20 minutes to get everyone down the aisle of the church. Then, the pastor preached a sermon about marriage. Yes, we were at a wedding so, of course, please share how God views marriage. It was heartfelt and moving and on point, but it took about 20 more minutes. Then, after a song, the pastor spoke of the symbolism of the ring. At this point, Brian started keeping track of the time.

The pastor spoke on what the rings mean, how they are made, why they are exchanged at wedding ceremonies and what they represent to the wearers and to the world. This took almost 25 minutes and then the pastor said to the groom, "What symbol do you bring?" Well, Brian leaned over and whispered in my ear, "Uh, a horseshoe?" We started giggling and then couldn't stop. I was so embarrassed, but that was probably one of the funniest things I had ever heard and we laughed until the pew shook. We certainly got some disapproving looks, but we honestly could not contain our giggles. I remember trying not to look at him and trying to think about dead animals and science tests so I'd stop laughing. To this day, we cannot attend a wedding without reliving that hilarious memory.

I had a friend at work whose parents lived on a farm. I told him the story of this wedding we attended and asked if he would be able to get his hands on a horseshoe for me. He delivered. This horseshoe is probably from the early 1900s. It was worn out and beat up. It was perfect.

I wrapped that horseshoe in a beautiful box with tons of fluffy tissue paper and a gorgeous bow. He did not have a clue and when he opened that box and saw that horseshoe he cried, which doesn't come easy. It is hanging in the hallway right outside our bedroom door to this day. It's a perfect reminder to us of a great fun memory, but the symbolism it holds for our relationship is priceless.

25

Restoration in our marriage was our first goal. Any couple that goes through an affair should be able to get help at their church to restore their marriage. We were also seeking reconciliation for Brian with the church. Reconciliation with the church would mean that Brian would be able to preach, teach, and hold positions of leadership again. This would take place later, after there has been much work done towards restoration. If restoration in the marriage is not being pursued, then reconciliation with the church should not even be considered.

Pastor Jim was committed to bringing Brian through a process of restoration and eventually, reconciliation with the church. Brian is very gifted as a teacher so to not utilize those gifts in the future would be a real shame.

Pastor Jim insisted that Brian and I get counseling, and I certainly could not live without my counselor. With our denomination, The Fellowship of Evangelical Churches (FEC,) there were a few procedures in place, but with Brian wanting to stay at Brookside Church, they honestly, in my opinion, didn't know what to do with him. Both of our counselors were willing to help to assist the church and denomination by setting up a process and walking us all through it. Setting goals and timeframes to move us toward restoration was not an easy undertaking.

I've talked with many wise people throughout this time and many are of the opinion that Brian should not be able to preach for a long time, if ever. I can appreciate this opinion because he had a leadership role in the church and he gave that up when he made the choice to be unfaithful. There are varying opinions on this and the timing of the reconciliation. I've come to believe that this should be determined by the couple's counselors, the leadership of the church, and the denomination they are involved in. Only after much prayer and consideration along with wise, Godly counsel should a person be able to be reconciled to the church. Again, to be clear, this is only to be able to preach, teach, or have a position of leadership in the church or ministry.

Pastor Jim met with Brian on a regular basis, asking him tough questions and making sure he was helping me to heal. Both Pastor Jim and Brian's counselor were adamant that he grant me the privilege of time. I was told several times that the time line was mine. If I wasn't ready to move forward, then it didn't happen.

This is a tough spot to be in, I'm sure. Many thought, or assumed, that under church leadership Brian and I were being taken care of, loved on, and counseled while moving through a process both to reconcile our marriage relationship and then Brian's relationship with the church. Through no one's fault, this was not happening. I love and will always love Pastor Jim. He invested so much into Brian and our family for years. However, I do believe he was too close to the situation. Jim kept the Elder Board posted on the progress Brian was making, and he kept the board and staff aware that things were also being taken care of by him.

Yes, Jim did meet with me a few times and he met with Brian many times. He held Brian accountable, but I believe he truly wanted to indicate to the church that things were fine and therefore, the healing process had been swept under the rug. I want to make this perfectly clear, Jim wanted us, the Clay family, to be able to heal in private. He also needed to fill the few roles that Brian had at the church. Jim, as the head pastor, had to move forward with the ministry of Brookside Church. This was not a slight to us, this was reality. When news of the affair broke, Jim didn't know what path Brian would take at this point. He didn't know what decisions I would make at this fragile time. He did know what needed to be done and that was to focus on Brookside Church. Again, I firmly believe that Pastor Jim had every intention of helping Brian heal and grow towards reconciliation with the church.

I believe that the announcement of Brian's "moral failing," was so pronounced that for the healing process to be so silent did a disservice to the church. A system or process of sorts would have benefitted everyone involved. It would have helped us know what to be working on. It would have given Pastor Jim guidance as to what steps to do next. It would have given the board, and the denomination leadership, a resource to follow Brian's progress as well.

In early Spring, about six months after the affair, Pastor Jim started to get sick. It was cancer that moved quickly and he passed away in July of that year. He was such a strong Godly man, and as my Pastor and my friend, I still miss him today. During Pastor Jim's sickness and death, many people approached Brian (in both sadness and anger) telling him that he should have been one of the leaders in the church to step up and lead during this time.

In the wake of this tragedy we were working hard to restore our marriage. Again, with the help of our counselors we were working every day to repair what was broken. Brian's reconciliation to the church, however, was put on hold.

I'll be the first to tell you that our church leadership moved our church through that very difficult time after losing Pastor Jim prayerfully and as best as they could. But, it is true that Brian most likely would have had many Sundays behind the pulpit preaching God's word to the people of Brookside Church. It was not to be.

About three months after losing Pastor Jim, Brian and I started wondering how this reconciliation journey would continue. Brian met with the church board, and they were under the impression that Pastor Jim had handled it and they believed we were further down the road to reconciliation with the church than we actually were.

By this time, we were 16 months out from the affair when Pastor Jim had laid the groundwork. Aside from counseling, we had not moved any closer to reconciliation with the church. And to be clear, reconciliation with the church would mean that Brian would be able to preach, teach and be in leadership in the church once again.

Generally, according to our counselors and our denomination, the process toward restoration and reconciliation would start within the first 48 hours to 2 weeks after the affair. This timeline would normally be defined by church leadership and the counselors involved. The couple would start with separate counseling, if possible, and accountability meetings with church leadership for the person who cheated. This is where they would be held accountable to think through and answer some pretty tough questions. The church leadership would communicate progress to the church board as well as the denomination. This is obviously different for each unique situation.

When Rocky Rocholl, the president of our denomination and a good friend, received word that Brian had been unfaithful he was traveling on business. Rocky called Pastor Jim immediately and told him that whatever he or Brian and I needed from the Fellowship of Evangelical Churches (FEC) they were available. In the denomination bi-laws, the general procedure is to defer to the local church. The FEC is careful not to storm in and take over a situation like this, but it is also "sitting on GO" for the leadership to assist in any way needed. When Rocky spoke with Pastor Jim, he told Rocky that he was handling it. It would be understandable that this was not just a difficult time for Pastor Jim personally because of his love and respect for Brian but it was also a very difficult time for him as the leader of Brookside Church. Pastor Jim and the leadership had to convey to the congregation that although this had happened, Brookside was still strong and moving forward to continue its strong presence in the community. I believe the message that Pastor Jim and the leadership of Brookside Church was trying to convey at this time was, "Everyone loves Brian and we need to be praying for the Clays but Brookside Church is still here and our ministry is growing and strong."

I cannot stress enough the importance that churches and ministries have a plan in place so leaders have a starting point, and if something unforeseen happens that halts the process, it would be documented so someone else could pick up the ball and run with it to finish. Also, it would be great to have some sort of plan to assist people willing to work on their marriage after one partner has an affair, be this person in leadership or not. I believe that the timing of our healing and the process not being completed for 2 years was the way it was supposed to be in our situation. God taught us so much, not just about healing our relationship, but with healing publicly in the eyes of the church. This journey was tough, but I don't want it to be in vain. If sharing our story will benefit a couple or a ministry in making the healing process easier then, praise God. Leaders in the church have many responsibilities. I'm not saying that the ministry should stop to help a hurting couple, but if a plan is in place it would make it easier for leadership to follow that plan rather than re-create the wheel. It was public from the beginning; how much more would the church have benefited and grown to have seen glimpses of the healing process?

Brian finally went to Rocky and said, "What can we do to get this started again? I need closure, Jill needs closure and our church body needs closure." Rocky Rocholl, in his role as president of our church denomination, took the reins and started moving Brian through a process of reconciliation; holding him accountable, requiring things of him, and working through a Bible study with him. We are both very grateful for his leadership.

So many people are looking for help for their broken relationships. If it is known that there is a process available towards healing and reconciliation in our marriages people will want to be a part of that if they find themselves in a similar situation. A dear friend said to me,

"You know the problem with the church is when we have messy issues we want to sweep them under the rug and not have them be 'in the light.' Sin is ugly and we can't grow in our faith if we don't confront our sin."

So, when our sin is confronted, grace and love need to come from our church body and that happened for us at Brookside. Healing must then be promoted, pursued and celebrated.
This would have been so much easier if there had been a plan in place.

26

I learned so many things through this trial. I truly wish there was a program to walk thru to healing and restoration and for leaders, reconciliation. I realize that everyone's needs are different. Everyone grieves uniquely. I realize that our situation is unique in that one, we stayed together and two, we wanted to be reconciled to the church, but it was upsetting that there was not some sort of process or steps to follow. Do people really just drop off from the church when sin disrupts our families? Are we losing people from the church because there is no healing safety net in place to give comfort and direction? Do people just leave and find another place to worship and start all over? Couldn't history just repeat itself if the healing doesn't take place? I realize that this could happen again to me at any time. The results would be different for sure, but where could I land in the church? I know they have Divorce Care and prison ministries (that I would most definitely be a part of as I would be serving my murder sentence).

It's important to have a program for people learning what the new normal is for their families - to have stepping stones for healing in place, from healing to wholeness. I believe that is what we need to be prepared when life throws us a curve ball. I know they have affair recovery programs as well, but I firmly believe this needs to be in the church, with the church so everyone can heal together and people can witness the healing and give glory to God.

A church has an exit plan if there is a fire. It varies because it depends on where the fire happens in the building and where the people are in the building at the time of the fire. If there is a death in the congregation, there is a plan in place for funeral services, meals after the funeral, and the needs of the family members during that time. A plan is in place with options available for what the family needs and requests. A plan is in place for weddings. Generally, there is a liaison for the church that meets with the engaged couple and helps coordinate times, needs, and availability for the wedding day and the days leading up to the wedding. This allows for certain rooms for the wedding party to get ready in, and sound engineers to be prepared with the music and sound needs for the day. There is a plan in place with options for the specific desires for the wedding.

My point is, there are plans in place for many of the things we face in life. Shouldn't there be a plan in place for people dealing with adultery in their marriage? A plan for couples in the church to heal their marriages. Tools to help rebuild a solid relationship once again. And another plan for church leaders who want to heal and be effective ministers of the Gospel once again?

I'm thinking when many people deal with this type of situation in their lives, it blows up, and the family either separates or stays together only to find another church where people don't know their past. Or they all drift away from church. The people in the old church are robbed of seeing a healing experience. This is not to say that healing didn't take place. But, what if it didn't? Or the couple divorces and new families are started? How is this helping anyone? Now, to make my point clear, if people don't want help or restoration in their marriage that is their decision. That is truly between them and God, but having a plan in place that people can have access to if it's needed and wanted, who knows how many relationships could be saved?

Brian and I were willing to work and restore our relationship as well as work through the weeds even though we didn't have a plan available to us. Now we knew the basics, or figured them out. I went to counseling. He went to counseling. We eventually went to counseling together, but this was for our relationship. When it came to reconciliation with the church, there was very little available to us, especially as a church leader. I think it's time to come up with plan. If you never use a fire exit plan, praise God you never had a fire! If you never use a restoration plan in your church, praise God, you never had a leader commit adultery!

Now, I realize that every situation is different. Brian didn't get involved with another person at the church. If our situation would have involved another family at the church it would have been a completely different can of worms. Then you'd be dealing with two families. But, how great would it be for our church leaders if when approached about helping a struggling marriage they would have had an outline (at least) to follow to assist these people. Again, every situation is different, but much of the healing process through pain is the same.

27

Trenton and I both enjoyed watching The Bible series on TV that debuted in early 2013. We would record the episodes and watch them together. Although sometimes, Trenton would watch them first and then we'd watch together and he'd narrate for me. On the episode where David and Bathsheba meet, Trenton said, as the adultery part was getting close, "Mom, you don't have to watch this part if you don't want to." This broke my heart for a couple reasons. First of all, in his young life to have witnessed and lived through this in our family is awful. I hate that my children have had to deal with this. But, it also broke my heart that his sensitivity to me was that in tune. What a precious heart my son has, to want to protect me from that.

As I talked about before, the kids were really loved through this process by their teachers and coaches at the school. At that time, all three of our children were in different youth groups at the church. Sidney was in the Senior High youth group. Keaton was in Jr. High youth group (7-8) and Trenton was in what is called 56 (5th and 6th graders.) News of this "event" spread like wildfire through the church and community. I don't believe my kids deserve special treatment of any kind, but not one of my kids got a phone call, a card, an email or even an extra pat on the back that I know of saying, "I'm praying for you," or "I'm here if you need to talk," from any of the youth leaders at our church.

I would think with the rampant divorce rate in our country that this would be well learned and practiced by our youth leaders to reach out to kids who are "knowingly" going through hard times. I understand if things are kept private and secret that leaders aren't going to know of every issue going on in their youth's lives, but this was public. This, I believe, should be a normal practice at the very least modeled from the top down, for a head pastor to say to the youth pastor, "Remember to be reaching out to the Clay kids during this time, make sure they know they are loved and supported."

Frankly, I loved our youth pastors and workers, but this hurt. I don't think the kids knew any different, but knowing that my kids were being loved on from every direction certainly would have made me feel comforted and not so alone in this healing process. I'm all for keeping things normal and routine, and I know my kids just wanted to not think about our family mess every second of every day, but a phone call or a text saying, "We are praying for you today," would have meant the world to me as their mom. I understand it was easier to ignore it and not bring it up because it was so hard to talk about. But the kids knew that practically everyone knew of our situation; I don't think they believed that many people cared. I believe instead of

BEING the church for all five of us during this time, they DID church.

There is a sense of relief when things on the surface appear back to normal or business as usual, but I believe an opportunity was lost to build deeper relationships with my kids and the other kids in the youth group. Discipleship on a different level could have been modeled to all these countless young people. A dialog could have been started with other kids going through similar situations could have been ministered to as well.

Rocky made a very good point regarding the time immediately following the news of the affair. I became "safe" because people knew about our situation and to many people, I was approachable. And please know that I wanted to help people and still want to help people going through similar situations to not feel alone. If the healing part of this process would not have been "swept under the rug," Brookside would have become a safer place as well. I know this sounds like I want both privacy and attention at the same time. I felt that this situation being so public to begin with could have sparked a deeper sense of community within Brookside Church had the healing process, not just for us but for all broken people, been spoken of and made available to others. Brookside Church would have become more of a place for broken people to show their brokenness. It would have become a richer place of healing.

No matter the sin, no matter the shame, we can all heal together. Now, do not get me wrong! Brookside is an incredible place filled with broken people who find refuge and healing all the time, but if people could have heard or seen what was available, the level of this could have risen substantially. Keep in mind, it would have been easier to leave Brookside but we wanted to stay. We love our church. Like many church bodies, people put on their Sunday best and do church, but don't feel comfortable showing their flaws and weaknesses when this very thing is what the church should be, a safe place. The level of community and healing and compassion would go through the roof, in my opinion. Can you imagine?

28

Rocky and the leaders of the denomination put together a guideline as to what to expect from Brian as he worked to be reconciled to the denomination and our church. Regarding accountability, Brian and I would meet with Rocky and his wife, Sue 4-6 times a year. We met several times, often for dinner or going to a basketball game, or just spending time together. It was also suggested that we meet with a small group 4-6 times a year and at this time we were attending our small group every other week. Also, personal accountability meetings between Rocky and Brian were to take place every week. They often met for breakfast. Rocky would ask Brian the hard questions. These breakfast meetings were not always easy for Brian.

During these times of accountability with Rocky and Brian, the framework set in place by Rocky and the leaders of the FEC, the underlying basic questions to resolve in Brian's heart were:

1. What was this really about? (What is the core of that sin in Brian's life?)
2. How did I not have enough safeguards in place? (How, in the future, can I assure that I won't sin in this way again?)

These two questions were the focus as they tried to work through how this happened in the first place and how to prevent it in the future. Rocky then discussed these 5 reasons as a starting point to coach and lead a person in Brian's situation:

The 5 reasons, or ABCs, failure happens in a marriage are the following:

1. Accountability (had ceased to be accountable)
2. Belief (This will never happen to me)
3. Commitments (At work takes priority over commitment at home.)
4. Devotional Life (Ceased except in time of desperation.)
5. (More) Emotional Energy (In self-justifying than self-evaluation.)

Brian and I still attended our separate counseling sessions during this time where we would always ask their recommendations for growth towards Brian's reconciliation with the church. Brian and Rocky also met with the church board to discuss progress and the next steps as this is also a great point of accountability.

Many churches and ministries have guidelines and procedures in their belief statements and doctrines. I believe it's important for leadership in all ministries to review these guidelines often. Also, to allow the church body to know that these guidelines exist and are there to help ministry leaders guide hurting people through this process, whether they are in leadership or not.

29

Just over two years passed since the affair, and our family was brought before the church body during all three Sunday services. Rocky explained the process Brian and our family had gone through to come to a point of reconciliation with the church. Brian got up and read a letter to the church leaders and to the church as a whole. This letter admitted his sin and asked for forgiveness from his family, his church and his Lord. Then, the leaders of the church came up and prayed with us and for us as we continued to heal and praise God for the renewing, cleansing power of His blood.

This is Brian's letter from that morning:

"Good Morning. It is good to be with you. Over two years ago, I violated my covenant of marriage before God. Our Pastor, Jim Pearson, was bold enough to immediately confront me personally and I confessed. I am here with you, my Brookside family, no longer just filled with sorrow, regret and shame. Over the past two years, I have sought the forgiveness of God, my wife, Jill, my family, my friends and my church. I am here today to rejoice with you that God is good. That healing and restoration do happen in the church. It was just over 5 years ago that I stood here and preached on Hosea & Gomer. I taught on God's unconditional, unqualified and

absolute love. Over the past two years, I have experienced that. I have a wife who has stood by me. I have a family who has stood with me. We have had the love and support of an amazing group of friends. Allow me to say I found comfort at the end of Hosea in Chapter 14. It says, "O Israel, come back! Return to your God! You're down but you're not out. Prepare your confession and come back to God. Pray to him." Take away our sin; accept our confession. Receive as restitution our repentant prayers. Thank you."

It was an emotional day for many people. There was such an outpouring of love to all of us that day and in the days that followed. So many people expressed that they appreciated the courage it took for us as a couple and as a family to face this mess head on and seek reconciliation for Brian with the church. People need closure. We all need to see God's healing and grace. This day gave many people tangible evidence of this. It brought back the emotions of one of the most difficult times our family faced; to be in front of three large crowds of people made it a very overwhelming day. The tears in people's eyes and the hugs we received that day all meant so much. We realized, that it would also bring up the topic for all these people who were there in the beginning, as well as to introduce a whole new group of people to the situation that probably had no idea what we had been through because they were new to the church.

The power of forgiveness was and is amazing. Perfect strangers wept with us, loved on us and thanked us for being so bold to see this come to a positive end. Many people would have left the church and gone somewhere else where no one knew them and they could start over quietly. Well, again, we don't tend to do things the easy way.

The kids really grew from that day as well. They saw the process come to a close. They had seen so much pain and hurt during those years and for them to have their father publicly apologize, not only to our family but to our whole church, was very powerful. It was healing for them. All the kids have been very sensitive to me about this and it started a new wave of interesting, positive conversations about the church and how God forgives and forgets when we confess our sins.

30

My mom was diagnosed with cancer, Hodgkin's Disease, when I was a little girl. She fought and prayed and God answered her prayers to see my sister and me grow up. My sister and I would play doctor's office waiting room when other kids were playing restaurant and grocery store. My mom spent much of her time fighting cancer so she could see us grow up. She went into remission the first time when I was probably four.

I remember being in second grade overhearing my parents talking about the cancer being back and what the doctor's plans were for her. I started getting headaches. Really bad headaches. I had a couple of them at school and I remember my mom sitting me down with my sister and telling us, "I am not going to die." I never had another headache like that in my life. She was going to fight the cancer.

She did what the doctors told her to do and she prayed like crazy. We had her for another almost 30 years.

In 2008 my parents were planning a trip to Germany with my aunts and uncles, where they were going to visit the village my grandmother grew up in. Mom was so excited about this trip. About two weeks before the trip she was feeling really short of breath and winded most of the time. She would not normally go to the doctor about something like this but since she didn't want to slow everyone else down on the trip she went to get checked out.

The doctor put her on a heart monitor for 24 hours and the results were not good. Her aortic valve was shriveled and not functioning fully. They wanted to do a valve replacement right away. All those years before when she received radiation for the cancer her lungs and heart were damaged. The radiation therapy kept the cancer away and kept her alive, but the damage to her organs was extreme.

The doctors told her she shouldn't go on the trip. They explained to her that she would most likely end up in a German hospital if she went on the trip. They also said that once they got her all fixed up, she could plan another trip. They told her, "Germany will always be there."

Mom had surgery in September 2008. After the surgery, her heart was strong, pumping blood like it hadn't in who knows how long. Basically, her other organs went into shock. Her kidneys started shutting down and her lungs were filling with fluid. She was in ICU for over a month. Her heart beat was erratic so the decision was made to put a pacemaker in. This was a much less serious surgery than the first one, but proved to be fatal. My mom flat lined during this surgery, and they were able to bring her back but not without significant oxygen loss and damage to her brain.

She passed away on November 2, 2008. I miss her every day. I really needed my mom when I was in the trenches fighting for my marriage. But I'm sort of glad she didn't have to be around to witness the pain and hurt during that time.

Growing up in a Christian home there were many things that were instilled in us. My parents instilled in us a desire to know and to serve God. It wasn't a list of Don'ts; it was a relationship with Jesus Christ that led to decisions on how to live. We were involved in church and I loved going to church. I loved going to AWANA and memorizing Bible verses. In High School I was very involved in youth group where I began to learn that God has no grandchildren. I wasn't going to heaven because my parents had a personal relationship with Jesus Christ. I, myself, needed to grow in my own relationship with Jesus Christ.

As a young girl, I knew that God loved me and sent His son to be my personal Savior. There are many distractions in this world (understatement of the year). When I was in 2nd grade, we had a couple that taught our Sunday school class. We were told to call him Big Daddy and every week he would share with us about Jesus and His love, and then ask if anyone wanted to ask Jesus into their hearts. I raised my hand probably 5 times that year. You can never be too sure, right? I would pray to ask Jesus to come into my life and to forgive me of my sin. I know that I only needed to ask once, but the assurance I received (along with most every other child in that class) by responding so often was a stepping stone for me to have the assurance that God now lived in me.

31

I was a follower of Jesus Christ from a very early age. I was taught the truths of the Bible and began to see the difference in the world and the way many viewed God and Christians. These are the truths that sustain me every day as well as during this difficult trial.

1. God wants us to be in relationship with Him. Sin got in the way. God sent His son, Jesus, to bridge the gap for us to God. Romans 3: 10-12 and 3:23 say, **"No one is righteous—not even one. No one is truly wise; no one is seeking God. All have turned away; all have become useless. No one does good, not a single one."** For everyone has sinned; we all fall short of God's glorious standard.

2. The consequence for our sin is death states Romans 6:23, **"For the wages of sin is death, but the free gift of God is eternal life through Christ Jesus our Lord. Jesus Christ paid the price for our sin, stated in Romans 5:8 But God showed his great love for us by sending Christ to die for us while we were still sinners."**

3. Through faith in Jesus Christ, we receive the free gift of salvation and eternal life. Romans 10:9-10, and 13, **"If you confess with your mouth that Jesus is Lord and believe in your heart that God raised him from the dead,**

you will be saved. For it is by believing in your heart that you are made right with God, and it is by confessing with your mouth that you are saved..."

4. For "Everyone who calls on the name of the Lord will be saved." Salvation through Jesus Christ brings us into a relationship of peace with God. Romans 5:1, **"Therefore, since we have been made right in God's sight by faith, we have peace with God because of what Jesus Christ our Lord has done for us."**

Romans 8:1,

"So, now there is no condemnation for those who belong to Christ Jesus."

Romans 8:38-39,

"And I am convinced that nothing can ever separate us from God's love. Neither death nor life, neither angels nor demons, neither our fears for today nor our worries about tomorrow—not even the powers of hell can separate us from God's love. No power in the sky above or in the earth below—indeed, nothing in all creation will ever be able to separate us from <u>the love of God</u> that is revealed in Christ Jesus our Lord."

32

As I grew up I learned more and more what a relationship with Jesus looked like. He wants to be close to us. He wants us to pray and study. He wants to reveal Himself to us and to guide us, but we have to be willing.

My grandparents on my mom's side were farmers in Northern Wisconsin. They had seven children, the youngest being my mom. My grandparents loved the Lord and prayed for all of us. I don't mean just a little. I mean a lot and often. There were twenty-one grandchildren spread out over the country, and they prayed for God's guidance and protection over us all. They committed themselves to pray for their family. This legacy of prayer has and continues to bless all of us. I know my mom's sisters and brother carried on this legacy with their families and grandchildren.

It's an understatement to say how blessed I am personally by the prayers of my grandparents, parents, aunts and uncles, and cousins because I know I may never know the vastness of the prayers prayed on my behalf. I can't imagine all the dangers I never encountered because of God's answered prayers. It is our privilege to pray for one another. My daughter said to me the other day, "What do you think my husband will be like?" I said, "I don't know, but I've been praying for him for years,"

The following verses in Colossians 3:1-17 really speak volumes to me. After this all happened, all the healing was focused on Brian, as far as what he needed to do to get right with God. Where had he failed? Where did he go wrong to get himself in this situation? The danger was falling into this "finger pointing" phase that would not be healthy for anyone. I had to continually and constantly make sure that I was working on my relationship with God too. I had to stay diligent and focused because wouldn't Satan have a heyday if I decided to make selfish bad decisions myself? I had to remain centered and in tune with what God was doing in Brian's life, but in my life as well.

"Since, then, you have been raised with Christ, set your hearts on things above, where Christ is, seated at the right hand of God. Set your minds on things above, not on earthly things. For you died, and your life is now hidden with Christ in God. When Christ, who is your life, appears, then you also will appear with him in glory.

Put to death, therefore, whatever belongs to your earthly nature: sexual immorality, impurity, lust, evil desires and greed, which is idolatry. Because of these, the wrath of God is coming. You used

to walk in these ways, in the life you once lived. But now you must also rid yourselves of all such things as these: anger, rage, malice, slander, and filthy language from your lips. Do not lie to each other, since you have taken off your old self with its practices and have put on the new self, which is being renewed in knowledge in the image of its Creator. Here there is no Gentile or Jew, circumcised or uncircumcised, barbarian, Scythian, slave or free, but Christ is all, and is in all.

Therefore, as God's chosen people, holy and dearly loved, clothe yourselves with compassion, kindness, humility, gentleness and patience. Bear with each other and forgive one another, if any of you has a grievance against someone. Forgive as the Lord forgave you. And over all these virtues put on love, which binds them all together in perfect unity. Let the peace of Christ rule in your hearts, since as members of one body you were called to peace. And be thankful. Let the message of Christ dwell among you richly as you teach and admonish one another with all wisdom through psalms, hymns, and songs from the Spirit, singing to God with gratitude in your hearts. And whatever you do, whether in word or deed, do it all in the name of the Lord Jesus, giving thanks to God the Father through him."

I believe and know that God is the final judge. He is the one who knows the hearts of every human being that has ever lived. I praise Him because He knows my heart; He loves me and still died for me to save me from my sins. I know that He knows Brian's heart. He knows his desires, his hurts, his sins and still loves him so much that He died for him. If God can forgive me, I must try to forgive anyone who sins against me. Please understand, if Brian didn't want to work on our marriage and didn't want us to have a future together, I would have accepted that. When faced with his remorse and his brokenness, I could have said, "No. I can't do this, I can't forgive this," and it would have been ok. God would have provided a way for me and the kids. He would have helped me heal. Brian wanted forgiveness, so I had to make a decision one way or the other. I chose to forgive and to heal. Sometimes I believe it would have been easier to divorce and start over. Somehow, I don't normally tend to do things the easy way.

Francesca Battistelli lyrics: "It's Your Life"

This is the moment
It's on the line
Which way you're gonna fall
In the middle
Between wrong and right
But you know after all
It's your life
Whatcha gonna do
The world is watching you
Everyday the choices you make
Say what you are
and who your heart beats for
Its an open door
It's your life
Are you who you
Always said you would be
You can live the way you believe
This is your opportunity
To let your life be one that lights the way

This song encouraged me so much. As I felt the world was
watching. During the days right after I found out I would sit on our
couch pretty much frozen in thought. I would pray that God would
direct Brian. I would pray that my response to Brian would be what
God wanted.

33

The day I found out, I figured out who this woman was and got on Brian's Facebook page and instant messaged her. I said, "HI!" She answered, thinking I was Brian, with a huge "WELL HELLO!!!!" I then continued with, "This is Jill, Brian's wife. I want you to know that you helped my husband bring my family and me to the deepest darkest hell. Shame on you!" She immediately "un-friended" him and blocked Brian and me as well. Trust me! I looked. I found ways to find out what she was up to because again, at this point, knowledge was power for me. She is honestly the most fortunate woman on the planet because most normal people in this situation would have shouted her name from the rooftops. Everybody would know who she is and what she did with my husband.

I was tormented with sleepless nights and restlessness. I wrote the following four months after I found out about the affair:

Written 1.3.12: I am so mad tonight. I can't believe he did this to me. What a fool and what a fool I am that I would have defended him forever if he had said it wasn't true. And that woman......What kind of selfish woman does this and KNOWS he's married? Then, she comes into my house and does this? How does she sleep at night? How does he sleep at night?

WHY AM I THE ONE UP AT NIGHT TORMENTED BY THIS
DISASTER??? My heart hurts today. "Lord. Why? What purpose
does this serve?"

This song "Worn" by Tenth Avenue North was a really accurate
description of how I was feeling during this time:

I'm Tired I'm worn
My heart is heavy
From the work it takes to keep on breathing
I've made mistakes
I've let my hope fail
My soul feels crushed by the weight of this world
And I know that you can give me rest
So I cry out with all that I have left

Let me see redemption win
Let me know the struggle ends
That you can mend a heart that's frail and torn
I wanna know a song can rise from the ashes of a broken life
And all that's dead inside can be reborn
Cause I'm worn
I know I need to lift my eyes up
But I'm too weak
Life just won't let up
And I know that you can give me rest
So I cry out with all that I have left
Let me see redemption win

34

Romans 8:26 says, "**In the same way, the Spirit helps us in our weakness. We do not know what we ought to pray for, but the Spirit himself intercedes for us through wordless groans.**"

This is definitely how I got through this very dark, lonely time in my life. The Holy Spirit interceded for me. I remember crying and trying to pray but I literally couldn't put words together. I know God heard my heart in those times. What an amazing God we have to hear the prayers of our hearts.

In John 3:22-30, John the Baptist is explaining to the spiritual leaders that he is not the Messiah but that Jesus is.

"**After this, Jesus and his disciples went out into the Judean countryside, where he spent some time with them, and baptized. Now John also was baptizing at Aenon near Salim, because there was plenty of water, and people were coming and being baptized. (This was before John was put in prison.) An argument developed between some of John's disciples and a certain Jew over the matter of ceremonial washing. They came to John and said to him, "Rabbi, that man who was with you on the other side of the Jordan—the one you testified about—look, he is baptizing, and everyone is going to him."**

To this John replied, "A person can receive only what is given them from heaven. You yourselves can testify that I said, 'I am not the Messiah, but am sent ahead of him.' The bride belongs to the bridegroom. The friend who attends the bridegroom waits

and listens for him, and is full of joy when he hears the bridegroom's voice. That joy is mine, and it is now complete. He must become greater; I must become less."

These verses have always meant so much to me. When my mom was in the hospital for her heart surgery, I drove into town to be with her, my dad and sister. I prayed throughout that whole time that I would become less and God would become greater. That people could see Christ through my actions and my actions would not be my own but Christ's. It was my prayer that the icky selfish part of me would not be visible to my mom or my family, and that my sole purpose of being there was to help, pray and support my family. It was my desire not to make waves or make anything about me.

When Brian had his affair, I prayed the same prayer. I prayed that I could love him and forgive as Christ did, and this was definitely harder than it sounded. I didn't want to make this situation about me. I obviously had to heal and I'm definitely human, but I wanted my responses to be Christ's responses. Getting in to the day-to-day dealings with Brian was very uncomfortable and hard. Sometimes just having a conversation with him was hard because I didn't want to look at him that day. My emotions were all over the place and I started to get my emotions in waves. It was similar to a death simply because the huge emotions would ebb and flow.

35

My God is enough so I am enough!

I struggled with being enough throughout my life. Was I pretty enough? Was I smart enough? Was I athletic enough? Was I spiritual enough? Was I funny enough? Was I a good enough employee? Did I earn enough to help our family? Was I enough for my husband? Well, I am enough because I am a child of the King. His grace makes me enough. By the world's standards, none of us are enough. We are not pretty enough, nor thin enough. We are not rich enough, nor powerful enough. We are not connected enough. How is my God enough?

Let's start simply with the definition of Enough:

Adequate: as much as needed

As much as is bearable: as much or as many as can be tolerated

To the necessary extent: to an extent that is as much as is needed

Synonyms: sufficient – adequate – plenty – abundant – plentiful – ample

After adjectives and adverbs. You use enough after an adjective or adverb to say that someone or something has as much of a quality as is needed, which leads us nicely into the world's definition of enough…

What is the world's definition of enough?
Are you good enough? Are you rich enough? Are you pretty enough? Are you thin enough? Are you funny enough? Are you strict enough? Are you disciplined enough? Are you rested enough? Are you healthy enough? Are you informed enough? Are you smart enough? Are you ambitious enough? Are you paid enough? Are you happy enough? Are you generous enough? Are you educated enough?

Although these things in and of themselves are not necessarily bad goals to have, but we can and will drive ourselves crazy with pushing towards all the unrealistic benchmarks set up by the world.

ENOUGH ALREADY!

My God says "MY GRACE IS ENOUGH!!"

II Corinthians 12:9 says, "But He said to me: My grace is sufficient for you, for my power is made perfect in weakness. Therefore, I will boast all the more gladly about my weaknesses, so that Christ's power may rest on me."
So, really, it is not about us! God didn't make us to be enough on our own. We need him to make up the difference. His grace is

sufficient. His grace is enough! His power is made perfect in weakness. How cool is that??

Many bad things happen every day to believers and non-believers. I truly believe that God allows us to go through trials and good times too, to draw us closer to him. He wants to be our everything. He wants to be in a relationship with us. He wants to make up the difference! So, then we will give HIM all the glory.

Again, He says EVERYTHING happening around us is not to discourage us, but to bring us closer to HIM. **IT IS NOT ABOUT US!**

Many times in my life I have experienced what it feels like to not be enough, or to not have enough.

In 2008, I ran the Chicago Marathon. I had run four half marathons and thought I'd give a full marathon a shot before I turned 40 the following February. I was as prepared as I could have been. My goal was to finish, not to beat any Kenyans. I prepared for about 6 months and went to Chicago the night before.

The day was perfect, not stormy, but not too hot. There was not a cloud in the sky, and as beautiful as it was, this is exactly what did me in. I didn't have a hat. I didn't train with one and had been fine.

The sun beating down on my head for 4 hours was not a good thing, but I was hydrated and felt good, as good as you can feel running for 4 hours. You sort of end up running with the same people after the first few miles, and a few of the runners around me started falling or tripping. I realized that I was literally running at an angle and couldn't straighten out.

An officer pulled me off the course and told me to sit and hydrate before continuing. They had a line of runners sitting on a curb with cold wet towels on our necks and drinking Gatorades. Just minutes later a runner came towards us, lost her balance and collapsed on the street just a few feet in front of us. She hit her head and was bleeding a lot. She was unconscious. They medi-vac'd her out of there very quickly. The rest of us were transported to the finish line. No marathon medal for me. I was in view of the mile 23 marker. I was almost there. 3.2 miles remaining, but my race that day was over. I didn't have enough in me to finish that race. I probably could have finished but at what cost? I was THAT close, but I didn't have enough in me physically to finish that race. I was not enough.

I was NOT ENOUGH in my marriage. I was not enough, by the world's standards and by Brian's standards I was not enough.

God used and is still using this situation for His glory. Almost immediately He moved in a way that I never saw coming. Brian's parents are wonderful people, but they can be very overwhelming. I always got the sense that I was not good enough by their standards for their wonderful son. There was a lot of misunderstanding between us over the years. I really wanted a good relationship with them but couldn't seem to make it happen. I will tell you, the minute they learned of the affair they embraced me like never before and we clung to each other. A week had passed and I really had trouble with not knowing where Brian was at night. He was with a family friend but I knew I would feel better and sleep better with him in the house, even if it was the basement to begin with so I asked him to come back and sleep in the basement. The next morning Brian was coaching Trenton's soccer team and his dad came to the game. He had talked to Brian and knew that he was back home. He came up to me with tears in his eyes and said, "Thank you for inviting Brian back into your home. You are gracious, kind and forgiving."

Honestly, God gave me a new relationship with Brian's parents and I am so grateful for that. I think we have a greater understanding and love for each other than ever before.

As painful as it was my God met me there and gave me ENOUGH courage; ENOUGH strength and ENOUGH grace to get through each day, sometimes each hour. He didn't give me enough to get through the next three years because I wouldn't continue to draw close to Him. I would think I could do it on my own. He gave me enough, He made up the difference. I had to be willing and I had to show up, but He literally did the rest. He gave me words when I had none, He gave me wisdom for our kids and praise God, He gave me strength to move towards forgiveness and healing.

Again, THIS WAS NOT ME. Yes, I had to be willing. I had to show up and (less of me Lord, more of You) but HE DID THE WORK. And He continues to do the work every day.

Like the Israelites in the desert with the manna. God didn't give them enough for storage and canning and freezing, He commanded that they only take and eat what they needed for that day!
He wants us near Him, He wants to be our lifeline! We are not made to be enough!

I was working at the same company for a while when God started making it clear to me that I should look for something else. I prayed for a long time about this process and just asked him to make it obvious. I'm a slow learner so He would have to make it clear...don't open three doors and a window. Just ONE door, please, and I will willingly go through it. Brian is a financial advisor and after much prayer, I applied to be the same. He is very good at what he does, but this door was the only one wide open so I walked through it. Some seven steps in the interview process and a couple months later I was offered a job. First, I had to pass some tests. Securities tests are not easy, so I studied for weeks and my first attempt at passing the Series 7, I failed. "What Lord? I thought we were in this together." I was allowed to take it again which doesn't normally happen, and I passed.

I was then studying for the Series 66, which I might add, is written by attorneys. You need a 75 to pass and you get three shots to pass it because it is that difficult. After 6 more weeks of studying I failed with a 65. Another 4 weeks and I sat for the test and got a 72. Yes, friends, I missed it by 3 points!! 4 more weeks of studying. Brain numb by this point. Too old for this. I sat for the test ready to knock the world out with my mad financial advisor skills and I failed with a 73%, missing it by two percentage points.

I sat in that testing center looking up at the ceiling and saying (not audibly because that's against the rules…trust me, the better half of 2013 was spent studying and testing in these testing centers so I knew the drill) "Ok Lord, you brought me here to this point. You have my full attention!!" Isn't this where God wants us all the time? I didn't want to blink, afraid I might miss something, looking to God for my next step.

I was not smart enough, by the world's standards or by the test's standards, to pass that test. Knowing full well that if God wanted me to be a financial advisor, He would have come down and passed that test for me. He wanted my full attention and commitment to go and do and be whatever He wants me to be. Again, I just have to show up, but Lord, I don't know where to show up.

I wasn't enough for that job. I didn't have what it takes. I may never know the answers to why I went through that, but I was obedient, I showed up. God said to go and do my best and with God as my witness, I did. By the world's standards your best might not ever be good enough, but God asks us to be obedient to Him, to show up. I rest in that.

The list of deficiencies is long, but my God is enough because He makes me enough if I let Him!

Jesus said it all when He told us to pray: Give us this day our daily bread. This quote by Faith Baldwin says it all:
"That bread is not only material, it is spiritual; in asking for it, we ask for a sufficiency of strength, courage, hope and light. We ask for enough courage for the step ahead, not for further miles, enough strength for the immediate task or ordeal, enough material gain to enable us to meet our daily obligations. Enough light to see the path – right before our feet."

In Philippians 4:18-20, Paul is thanking the Philippian church for their gifts and their generosity. God supplied his needs through the church, **"I have received full payment and have more than enough. I am amply supplied, now that I have received from Epaphroditus the gifts you sent. They are a fragrant offering, an acceptable sacrifice, pleasing to God. And my God will meet all** your needs according to the riches of his glory in Christ Jesus. To our God and Father be glory for ever and ever. Amen."

What a mess our world is in, and it is so hard to block it out. Galatians 1:10 says, **"Am I now trying to win the approval of human beings, or of God or am I trying to please people? If I were still trying to please people, I would not be a servant of Christ."**

It truly is one or the other. Now, the wonderful thing is, if our goal is to please and honor God and we seek to do that, in the end those around us that we love, will be pleased as well.

36

Brian is many things; he is funny, charming, the life of the party and he has integrity. He has always commanded the room when he walks in. Before the affair, people loved when he preached because he was a straight shooter. You believed that he talked the talk and walked the walk. Many people put him up on a pedestal, including me. It was easy to do because he was too smart to do something so stupid. He knew the verse in Numbers 32, **"Be sure your sin will find you out."** He would make comments on how ridiculous some people were who tried to get away with sin in their life. He would always drive home the point of doing things "God's way" because it's always the right way. One family friend, who had loved Brian's teaching and had heard him speak countless times, shared with her mom that she didn't know what to believe anymore. Her mom told her, "Everything Brian taught you is still true."

I loved watching God bring people in, build relationships with each other and with God as they nurtured their growing families. I always felt that God had given me a front row seat to His ministry and life changing ways. Brian would preach and teach at our church as well as many area churches. He taught a Sunday School class for years and has an incredible gift of teaching. One friend once said to me,

"Brian has a way of making people laugh with their mouth open and then he shoves the truth down their throats." I'm pretty sure that's as accurate a statement there is to explain Brian's teaching style.

Brian had since left full time ministry and began working for Edward Jones. He is incredible at everything he attempts. He loves his work, and also has the flexibility to preach and teach which he loves as well. It really seemed like the best of both worlds. Brian was also coaching the kids in soccer, both fall and spring seasons, as well as basketball. I was busy. He was super busy. I thought we had a good thing going. I thought we had an understanding. I was wrong.

When this all came to light, I was of course devastated, but I had felt so safe in the integrity that Brian had. It was almost a double blow because he wasn't the man I thought I knew. You would think that you would get a glimpse of possibility, even in hindsight, but I saw nothing, no warning signs. I was so ready to jump to his defense and had he denied it, I would believe him still today.

There was a fear Brian had after he had the affair that I would have what he called, "a revenge affair." He kept bringing it up, telling me he doesn't know how he would he handle it if I would actually have an affair. Well, after asking so many times and bringing the topic up so many times I finally had enough. I realize this is not the way I should talk or the way I'd want my children to talk, but I said,

"Look, Brian, you need to realize that one d**k is more than enough in my life." He got the point.

37

Brian and I both grew up in conservative Christian homes. We both attended Christian High Schools. I graduated and started college at a school in Illinois. Brian graduated a year later and started at Anderson University. Halfway through my sophomore year I transferred to Anderson University in Anderson, IN., because of their broadcasting department. I had a boyfriend who would be graduating from college that spring. I remember the first time I met Brian. I had classes with one of his friends who one day I saw in the cafeteria. I stopped to say, "Hi." Brian was sitting across the table from him. He introduced me to Brian and then it got awkward. They started kicking each other under the table, like I wouldn't notice.

Our friends all seemed to be friends and we would often end up at the same places and parties. We had many mutual friends. The next semester in the fall, I broke up with my longtime boyfriend. It was hard for me because I did love him. I just knew that we were not supposed to be together forever. The evening I ended it on the phone I went to a friend's room and she prayed with me. She said, "Why don't you take a walk? Take a walk with someone you don't know, who doesn't know this past relationship. Go out and laugh a little. I have a perfect person for that. Let me call Brian and see if he'll take a walk with you." I said fine. She called Brian and he said, "No, wait, who is it? Jill Janavice? Tell her I'll meet her in her lobby in 10 minutes."

I wiped my tears away and went down to the lobby. In walked Brian and he said, "So we're taking a walk? I understand you just broke up with your boyfriend, are you pregnant?" I said," No, I'm not pregnant!" We obviously didn't know each other. We did walk that night. Although, I still question why I didn't kick him in the shin and run the other way. We talked and laughed. It was refreshing and the first of many late night walks around campus. He asked me to his social club's Christmas formal and I said yes. A week before the event, Brian had a friend drop off a letter to me that broke it off. I was hurt. I was mad, but I moved on to other fish in the college sea.

The next fall, I returned to school for my senior year. The mutual friend who had sent us on that first walk kept telling me that Brian was obsessed with me and wouldn't stop talking about me. I got a call from Brian one night and he said, "Jane* tells me you hate my guts. What's that all about? I know I hurt you last year, but I thought we were ok." I told him, "I never hated you. Never said I hated you. She said you are obsessed with me, like creepy obsessed. What's THAT about?" He said, "Wow. I think we're being played. Can we meet somewhere and talk?" We met at Taco Bell and talked until they closed. We have been together ever since.

Brian could always make me laugh. I never thought I had to carry the conversation. I didn't feel like I had to lead the relationship. We were partners, friends, a team. We had very similar beliefs, our faith was important to both of us. Having a personal relationship with Jesus Christ was paramount to every other relationship. I graduated the following spring and moved back to Illinois to find a job. Brian started his senior year at AU and also started working as a youth pastor at a church in Anderson, Indiana.

Around Thanksgiving of his senior year at Anderson University, Brian started having chest pain and shortness of breath. He went to the campus doctor and was told that he had a pneumothorax, a collapsed lung. Brian struggled through until Christmas, but couldn't take it anymore. His parents took him to the ER and they admitted him. He was in the hospital for two weeks and eventually had surgery to repair his lung. I went to visit him on New Year's Eve and spent the day at the hospital with him. I had to get back to work on January 2, so I went over to Parkview Hospital on New Year's Day.

As we were sitting together, he said, "What do you want when we get engaged? Do you want to be on the beach? Do you want to be in the mountains?" I said, "No, just surprise me." He leaned over to his night table and pulled out a ring and asked me to marry him. I'm pretty sure I said yes, but I couldn't hug him because of all of his tubes and stuff so I ran out of the room and told a nurse. She said, "Oh, how wonderful! Nothing good ever happens on the oncology floor." She hugged me and lifted me off the ground. (They were remodeling the pulmonary wing so all patients were moved to different areas of the hospital.) I ran back in the room and Brian said, "Is that a yes?" We had several hospital staff come visit to congratulate us and we even got a cake from the cafeteria that said, "Congratulations on the New Baby," with a body fluid bucket filled with ice and two 7ups.

Brian graduated in the spring and we were married on August 1st, 1992. I moved back to Anderson as Brian stayed on as youth pastor while I looked for a job.

38

There are three things a wise woman told me before we married that I will never forget: STUDY YOUR HUSBAND. Make it a point to learn about him, listen to him when he talks. Studying your husband makes you love him better. Don't look for the negatives or weaknesses; look for the things that drive him. Get his point of view on all sorts of things! You don't have to be June Cleaver, but if you see that he likes things a certain way, do it that way if it's possible! It will make him feel special, appreciated, and loved and will probably not take too much effort on your part.

My dear husband only likes white hangers in his closet. Normal? No. But, he likes it that way. Does it drive me crazy when I'm doing laundry to make sure all of his clothes get hung on white hangers? Of course, but in view of eternity is it a big deal to do that for him? NO. STUDY him. Look for the simple likes and dislikes; it will help you love him better!

Sometimes I have to remind myself of all the good stuff about Brian. He is the busiest person I know. He goes from meetings to coaching one of the kid's teams, then back to a meeting at church or to teach a class. We usually don't see him for long on any given day. Praise

God, he is at church helping people and I thank God that he has a job that can support our family. Talk your husband up to other people! And tell HIM! Tell him occasionally what you love about him! Don't forget the good stuff!! You need to remember it and he needs to hear it!

I just told Brian out of the blue yesterday that I think he is pretty great. He looked at me like he was waiting for the punchline. This is not good. I obviously need to tell him more often that I'm glad he is my husband and I'm glad we are in the fight together.

SEEK TO UNDERSTAND, NOT TO BE UNDERSTOOD. This is a tough one. We are all very self-aware in this world. Okay. We're selfish! I tried to understand him, and it was not so easy, but the focus was off ME and MY NEEDS. Empathy goes a long way. Through all of this, I realize and want to point out that our relationships are two-way streets. I'm not saying to surrender who you are in your marriage and be a doormat, but, when I stop focusing on myself, my world gets a lot bigger and I can see the good stuff more clearly!

PRAY for your husband. It's amazing how your outlook changes when you start to see things through God's eyes. Prayer often will not change the person you are praying for, but it will always change your heart.

I was always so relieved that Brian and I didn't have past sexual partners to be concerned with. I was happy that we had both waited to have sex until our wedding night. I always thought how difficult it would be to run into his ex-girlfriends if they had had sex and how awkward it might be. I am so grateful I didn't have to face that until 19 years into our marriage.

39

Now, I have to wonder if this woman is lurking at the mall and if she sees me before I see her. Don't get me wrong. She's not looking for me. I believe she would be equally horrified to see me face to face. I wonder about all the things she knows about me after being in my home with my husband. I don't believe I've ever met her but there are some things I know about her.

I did some Facebook stalking and figured out who our mutual friends are, where she works and what side of town she lives on. In the early days of discovering this I figured she knew a heck of a lot about me and that knowledge was power, so I did some digging of my own. I know that she lied to her family about being the one guilty of this. I know she called Pastor Jim and confessed and wanted to meet with him and apologize to him. He told her to go to her own pastor and she told him that if she did her father would find out and he would be devastated. Really? If you cared so much about what people think then what are you doing sleeping with other people's husbands in the first place? She asked Pastor Jim if she could meet with me and apologize. What? You want to ease your own conscience after helping to destroy my life as I knew it? No way, Babe! I told Pastor Jim, "I have not slept in a month and she wants me to ease her conscience so she can sleep at night? "No way!" Pastor Jim agreed and passed on the word to her.

I have no idea what kind of woman could do this to another woman. One fear I had was that she would come and boil my bunny like in the movie "Fatal Attraction." My counselor told me she believed she wasn't that kind of woman. This damaged woman responded to men the way they responded with no emotional attachments. Sex was just sex in her eyes as well, just a cheap thrill, and selfish. Not caring who was affected by her actions.

For a long time and honestly, sometimes still, she is the third person in our bedroom. She haunts my thoughts. "Did he do this with her?" "Did she do this better than me?" "Was he more satisfied with her?" I hate these thoughts, but the only way I can combat them is with prayer. I have prayed her out of my mind on countless occasions. The nightmares, on the other hand, are awful. They still come sometimes.

Someone once asked me if I thought Brian had been trapped into committing adultery to bring down the ministry he was involved in, and I recall saying, "This was no trap. He set out to get sex and he brought this into our marriage. He set the trap himself."

I believe that if she had said no he would have found someone else to commit adultery with, so as much as I want to hate her for being an active participant, he used her as well. He went out of his way to find someone willing and he did. He told himself lies that he deserved this, and worked up in his head a hatred for me as a justification to follow through with his selfish desire. This was not a sin of taking advantage of an opportunity that falls in your lap. This was going out of your way to commit sin, hopefully, that no one would find out about.

A huge part of me wanted to expose who this woman was, but for some reason we have kept it a pretty tight-lipped secret. I think this is mainly because she is not the focus of the issue. She was a willing part of it, but she doesn't deserve to be a part of the healing. I don't know if she is still committing adultery.

I do know that she is quite fortunate that I am the one who is going through this because I believe I've been more than gracious by not dropping her name all over town like a bad habit. For a long time, I needed to know if he still wanted her or thought about her, but I learned that I had to give that up to God as quickly as the thought formed in my head. I had to focus on what I knew to be true and stand firm on those promises.

Before the affair, I thought we were through the hard parts of our marriage. The struggles were real. We had a set a pace and had an understanding. I was wrong. I wrote this a few weeks following: I can't believe it's been 22 days since my life changed forever. It feels like a dream still. I'm so tired of thinking about this mess, but I know I need to go through the muck and fog or I'll never get past it.

Brian had an appointment a few months after D-Day. It was at 6pm at his office. He was not home at 8:00. I started to freak out a bit. He didn't answer his office phone or his cell phone. I tried his cell again a few minutes later and he answered; he was still in a meeting. I wanted to trust him, but the bank was empty.

I also wrote a few months out: Getting intimate but don't know if its healing or trying to make him not go somewhere else. I want to meet his needs and I want to be his everything but I know I can't be. For years, I've struggled with not being enough for him, socially, sexually, spiritually. Well, it is true, but what if it happens again? I witnessed a miracle. My marriage is that miracle. I truly am a miracle. Praise God! He gets all the glory. I know right as we began to heal, Brian would listen to me. He would hear me and try to understand my viewpoint on everything. We had some great productive conversations. Sometimes I wonder if he will wander again. I remember he told me back then that he would never cheat on me again. I told him, "But you were never going to cheat on me in the first place." The promise, unfortunately, doesn't mean as much to me the second time around. I understand he has needs. He is very concerned with his needs. I have needs too. He thinks that there is something wrong with me that I don't want to be intimate with him all the time. Well, it doesn't mean I don't love him or desire him. It simply means my needs are different. I need to be heard. I need to be cherished.

Let your prayer be, "God must become greater, I must become less."

I am not a Theologian. I am not a Counselor. I am not a teacher, nor a psychiatrist. I am simply a woman who loves God and my family. I honor marriage because God ordained it. I think divorce is right in many situations. I just know it was not for me in the situation that I was faced with. I believe that marriage is a covenant set up by God. I had every right both in the world's eyes and in the view of the Bible to divorce my husband. When faced with our situation AND seeing that he was remorseful and repentant to both God and me, I chose to stay and fight for our marriage. It was not and is still not easy.

40

We moved to Fort Wayne in 1995 when Brian was asked to be a youth pastor in New Haven, Indiana. A year and a half later, we had our first precious baby, Sidney Lin. She is hilariously funny, driven, outrageously competitive, and committed to Jesus Christ. Nineteen months later, we welcomed her little brother, Keaton Douglas. Our hearts were blessed and our hands were full. He is just as funny, equally as competitive, so talented, and a delight to be around. He, too, has a tender heart for Jesus. Two and a half years later Trenton Michael rounded out our family. He is kind hearted, witty, God loving, and so easy going. God has blessed us with these precious, healthy wonderful children. I'm very thankful for them every day.

My kids are growing up in a different, rougher, tougher world than I grew up in. Much of my growing up years were spent in church, Sunday School and Awana Clubs. I'm so grateful that my parents saw fit to build a strong foundation in my life and heart that is based on God's Word and His love for me. I know that this was my parents' desire, but I also realize that it was up to me to make the decision to follow God on my own. I had to decide for myself if I would embrace His truths in my own life.

Satan desires to get a foothold in the Christian community every chance he gets. If we are not proclaiming God as our Savior but are living for ourselves and doing whatever we desire, Satan leaves us alone. If we are claiming to be Christians, Satan comes full speed to try and derail us. We are targets, walking targets every day. We need to be praying targets. We need to pray protection around our spouses, our kids, our friends, and our pastors and leaders every day!

I do believe that putting our kids in a Christian school is a wonderful thing, but they face the heat more than ever because Satan wants to take down the school as a whole. We are essentially putting a target on their backs as well.

I am on the school board at my kids' school and I was unsure about being part of it in the beginning because I didn't know what I could offer to the school at the board level. I had a conversation with a friend who was just moving off the board when I was moving onto it. He said, "Jill, you have to realize that when you put yourself in a position where you are claiming your faith publicly and serving in this capacity, Satan is going to attack. He is going to try to bring you down. Be wise and be careful. Be prayerful." I'm not sure that wiser words have ever been spoken to me. I had my first board meeting on Monday, August 8, 2011, and I found out about Brian's affair on Friday, September 2, 2011.

God called me to be on the board. I do not take it lightly. I pray for the board members, our administration, and our school all the time. It's my honor to do that.

Mark Batterson, an author I really admire, wrote in his book, <u>In A Pit With A Lion On A Snowy Day,</u> about how David, a shepherd boy, had the main job of protecting his sheep. If wolves or any animals came his way and threatened his sheep, he would use his slingshot to injure or kill these predators. He did this everyday - all day long. He had target practice. He had a simple weapon, a rock and a slingshot, but he was a pro at using it.

When God called him to slay Goliath, he might not have felt ready, he might have felt small and weak. God called him and he knew what to do. He had practiced his aim for years. This was not a surprise to him. He knew he could hit his target right between the eyes. I love the way Mark Batterson explained this in his book. God is preparing each of us every day for the future. It might seem mundane, even boring, but God is preparing us for battle. If we let Him.

God was preparing me for what was going to happen in my life. He was getting me ready to stand for him. I honestly don't know how people handle life without the hope of our Savior. I don't know how people go day to day without Him, His grace and His guidance.

The world changes every day, but my God is the same yesterday, today and forever. The more in prayer and in His Word that I am, the more I see him working all around me and bringing me opportunities to share about Him. It's amazing how my perspective changes when I seek to view people through God's eyes instead of my own. Trust me, this is not easy, especially when faced with huge disasters in our lives.

41

God told me in many ways that He wanted me to write this book. He wanted me to share about getting blindsided and remaining faithful. He wanted me to share my story. He had me lead a Bible study at church on The Circle Maker by Mark Batterson. This is the second time I've led this study and probably the fourth time I've read the book. In the book the author shares how he was supposed to write the book, In A Pit with a Lion on a Snowy Day, and that God kept pressing it on his heart. God told him to set a date for completion. During this study, I was writing a lot and had really been making progress but I was also working full time and was just busy with life. I felt challenged by the author's story in The Circle Maker, but also by the ladies in the study. One of them said, "Have you set a deadline?" No. I hadn't. She said, "Well, you better get to it."

The next week they made some changes at work and I was out of a job. I don't believe in coincidences. Yes, it stung. I really liked my job and the people I worked with. I didn't see it coming. I felt wronged. But God gave me this verse and a wake up call to write this book!

John 16:33 **"I have told you these things, so that in me you may have peace. In this world, you will have trouble. But take heart! I have overcome the world."**

On my way home the day I lost my job, I called Brian to tell him I was let go. He said, "We will figure it out. We will be fine." Thank you, Brian. That means so much because we have been through worse, but God always carries us. When I get home, I see that my oldest son is the only one home. My little dog is so happy to see me and attacks me with love as I walk in the door! She has no idea how much she's going to see me from now on! I then go upstairs to tell Keaton what is going on. He is upset for me, but promises to pray for the situation. What an amazing kid he is.

Then I get a text from a friend from work who saw this whole thing go down. She says she's coming over to talk. Brian has a late meeting, and when my friend gets to my house I tell her that I have to go pick up my youngest son, Trenton, from work, so why don't we eat there? She agrees and we go to tell Trenton the news. He is so sweet. He tells me those people are crazy for letting me go, and then we eat.

After some cheese curds for my wounded spirit, we go home try to try to figure out what happened that day and what led up to it. We laugh a lot and when my friend gets up to leave I say, "Oh. Wow. Why do you have to leave?" She says, and I will always remember, "Well, some of us have to work in the morning!" I laughed until I cried, and Trenton was still laughing about it the next morning!

That next morning, I looked at my phone and see that I have received a call from another bank where I had applied to the week before on a whim, and I also received a call from a representative from a publishing company interested in what my book was going to be about. Really? How can I feel like a loser when God is shining so brightly in my life?

Apparently I need to get about the business of writing this book. God is giving me the words and obviously the time to do so is now. He has my attention.

"He has showed you, O man, what is good. And what does the LORD require of you? To act justly and to love mercy and to walk humbly with your God." This is found in Micah 6:8, and is still a constant reminder of what God asks of us on a daily basis.

God's Word is alive and He kept laying many verses on my heart during this time.

Hebrews 3:14 says, "We were sure about Christ when we first became His people. So let's hold tightly to our faith until the end."

Hebrews 11.1 says, "To have faith is to be sure of the things we hope for, to be certain of the things we cannot see."

Psalms 18:1-2: "I love you, LORD God, and you make me strong. You are my mighty rock, my fortress, my protector, the rock where I am safe, my shield, my powerful weapon, and my place of shelter."

42

Brian and I started attending Brookside Church in January of 1998. Sidney was one and I was pregnant with Keaton. We were not very involved yet because my husband had been a youth pastor at our previous church and we were just finding our way back into ministry, plus we also had a young family.

The next year I was invited to go on a women's retreat with a friend. I agreed to go and then at the last minute she couldn't attend because of a family emergency. I was not going to go when Linda Pearson got wind of this and said, "That's it, you are rooming with me!" Ok, the pastor's wife would know if I left early or didn't show up at all! But, I went anyway!

I really enjoyed myself, but in a conversation with Sue Rocholl, whom I didn't know at all before that weekend, kept talking about MOPS and how Brookside needed a MOPS group. Finally, I asked the question that would change my life, "What is MOPS?" She described it as a group of women who meet, usually in a church, to get a break from their preschoolers to eat a warm breakfast, hear an informative speaker, and connect with other Mothers of

Preschoolers. It sounded wonderful to me and I asked why she couldn't start one herself and she said… "A mother of preschoolers has to start it," and she was past that stage.

Would you believe that I didn't sleep very well the next two weeks? All I could think about was that conversation with Sue about MOPS. Remember, I had never even been to a MOPS meeting. So, I found Sue at church, and thanked her for keeping me awake for two weeks and asked what we needed to do to get started?

The next Sunday in church, our worship leader shared some powerful words that God was ready to use us and we just had to be ready to be used. He said, "Who of you is ready? Who is going to say, I'll go, Lord?" He hadn't asked anyone to stand for the song, but I found myself standing up. I found myself standing up, singing and crying, saying, "Yes, Lord, I will do what you will have me to do."

I found out later that a number people had stood up during that song, but at the time I felt it was just God and me. I will never forget the day he called me to lead MOPS. I was so blessed to be a part of that prospering ministry. He grew me, stretched me, moved me and gave me a front row seat to His miracles at work in the hearts of the moms at Brookside Church MOPS. I knew that even if I didn't feel equipped to do this that God was in it and He would do the hard work.

There were struggles getting this group together and considering I had never been to a MOPS meeting, there was quite a learning curve for me. Two wonderful ladies teamed up with me to start our MOPS journey and amazingly, many women showed up to that first MOPS meeting at Brookside Church in October of 1999.

I learned many things about myself and other people, but the one major lesson I learned is that God changes lives! He loves us so much at every stage of our life. He is in the details. He cares about us, every thought, every diaper change, every sleepless night. He is here and He loves us.

I know that God used the relationships and friendships from MOPS to bring me closer to Him. Two of my three best friends I met because and only because of MOPS. I'm so grateful for the journey that God put me on. He definitely doesn't call the equipped. He equips the called. Thank God He called me!

43

While in a truly amazing Beth Moore study on the book of Revelation, I learned so much and I really appreciated her research and love of God's word. I was BLOWN AWAY by a verse that we studied.

In 2 Corinthians 1:21 – 22 it says, **"Now it is God who makes both us and you stand in Christ. He anointed us, set his seal of ownership on us, and put his Spirit in our hearts as a deposit, guaranteeing what is to come."**

I just love this. When we make the decision to follow Him, He sends His Spirit to place a deposit in our hearts. We are His and His alone. He will come back and claim us! It's like the God of the universe said, "Jill Clay's heart? Dibs! She's mine!" I can't get enough of this verse. He is so intensely interested in my life, the state of my heart, that He knows the number of hairs on my head right at this minute (Luke 12:7 and Matthew 10:30). The God of the universe has me in the palm of His hand and LOVES me. This is an amazing, awe-inspiring thing. He loves us!

Jesus loves me, this I know
For the Bible tells me so
Little ones to Him belong.

I am weak but He is strong.
Yes, Jesus loves me.
Yes. Jesus loves me.
Yes, Jesus loves me
The Bible tells me so.

Jesus loves the little children
All the children of the world.
Red and yellow, black and white they are precious in His sight.
Jesus loves the little children of the world.

Please forgive the jaunt to three-year-old Sunday school, but how incredible are these little songs? These are so powerful in their meaning for all of us, but so understandable to sweet little children of all ages.

I know my marriage is stronger than it was four and a half years ago. Would I go through this all again? That's a good question. I was pretty happy with life back then, but if it means that God will be glorified by who we are today then, I say, "YES." I would go through it again. In Genesis 50:20, Joseph tells his brothers who sold him into slavery, **"You intended to harm me, but God intended it for good to accomplish what is now being done, the saving of many lives."**

We've been given many powerful illustrations of what the church should look like in the Bible. Another beautiful picture of this was brought up in our Sunday service recently. The tale of the Good

Samaritan is a parable and many have opinions on who the symbolism of the different characters represents. This parable is taken from the book of Luke 10:25-37,

"On one occasion an expert in the law stood up to test Jesus. "Teacher," he asked, "What must I do to inherit eternal life?"

"What is written in the Law?" he replied. "How do you read it?"

He answered, "'Love the Lord your God with all your heart and with all your soul and with all your strength and with all your mind'; and, 'Love your neighbor as yourself.'

"You have answered correctly," Jesus replied. "Do this and you will live."

But he wanted to justify himself, so he asked Jesus, "And who is my neighbor?"

In reply Jesus said: "A man was going down from Jerusalem to Jericho, when he was attacked by robbers. They stripped him of his clothes, beat him and went away, leaving him half-dead. A priest happened to be going down the same road, and when he saw the man, he passed by on the other side. So too, a Levite, when he came to the place and saw him, passed by on the other side. But a Samaritan, as he traveled, came where the man was; and when he saw him, he took pity on him. He went to him and bandaged his wounds, pouring on oil and wine. Then he put the man on his own donkey, brought him to an inn and took care of him. The next day he took out two denarii and gave them to the innkeeper. 'Look after him,' he said, 'and when I return, I will reimburse you for any extra expense you may have.'

"Which of these three do you think was a neighbor to the man who fell into the hands of robbers?"

The expert in the law replied, "The one who had mercy on him."

Jesus told him, "Go and do likewise."

Our pastor was talking about how we are that injured, robbed and beaten man, and Jesus is the Good Samaritan. Jesus tends to our wounds and brings us to the innkeeper. Then, He pays for our stay. He returns later to pay our debt to the innkeeper. The church is the inn. We are to tend to injured people. We are to help them heal in safety and love. We are to provide rest for the weary and broken. This is such an accurate picture of what the church is supposed to be.

Building trust back into our relationship is a topic that many have asked me about and like everything, this is a journey. The first day I learned of the affair, obviously, all the trust up to that point was blown to smithereens. I didn't know what to believe. I didn't know if I could trust Brian's friends, his office assistants, etc. Had they all been in on this?

Brian stayed at our friends' house on that very first night in September, 2011. I knew where he was and knew the people he was with, which was, obviously, very important to me. The nights that followed, Brian stayed at an acquaintance's home. This single man was very gracious to let Brian stay there for a week. I remember Brian calling me from there and having this friend get on the line to verify that he was there with him. I found out later that this man and Brian really hashed through a lot of things, which was very good for him. I struggled because I didn't want Brian in the house, but I went a little crazy when I didn't know where he was, especially in the middle of the night.

Brian was very good at calling me from land lines to let me know where he was and who he was with. Realize, I didn't know what to believe, who to trust, and who knew what or who at this point. I don't remember being the one asking for these calls from land lines just to ease my mind a little, but whoever thought of it, it did help during this unrest. After a week, I asked Brian to come see the kids and stay for dinner because all these wonderful people had dropped off delicious meals all week and we needed help eating it. Over dinner that night I told Brian that I might feel better if he came home and stayed in the basement.

A counselor friend of ours spoke to both of us regarding this at length. I remember him saying that me asking him to come home, even to the basement, is a huge step and that I can't renege on it later. He was saying that if I ask Brian home now he doesn't want me to change my mind in two weeks and say, "Forget it. You need to leave again." I really took that to heart because I certainly didn't want to go backwards, but I hated not having him in the house. It was better for me, and I slept better (maybe the Ambien had something to do with that too.) It was definitely better for the kids as well.

Early on, Rocky had a good conversation with Brian about this very thing. He asked Brian a really good question, something like this: "Brian, it's great that you are back in the house, but what if Jill has you live in the basement for seven years? Is that going to be ok with you?" I still don't actually know how, or if, Brian answered that question, but it was a thought provoking one. At the time I couldn't stomach the idea of Brian being back in our bed. I didn't know how long it would take to move him up from the basement. Some days it seemed like it would be in a month or two, and other days I wanted him in the basement for years.

Every day was a new day. Some days I felt okay, and other days I didn't believe a word he said. I really went through a grieving process for our old relationship.

44

Brian was very good about checking in with me during the day. Another thing his counselor told him was that he had to answer every question I asked him. I don't think I "over used" this, but he might think differently. I asked Brian things about his day, about his thoughts, and he answered each and every question.

I remember asking him if he heard from the other woman or saw her at all. I would ask if he thought about her. I would ask if he missed her. Did he dream about her? I would also ask what Scripture verses have hit home with him lately. What made him laugh today? I don't think they were all questions that were hard to answer, but it felt as if I was getting to know him again, if that makes sense. Some of the answers were hard to hear, but I asked the questions so I had to be prepared to hear the answers regardless. This helped build trust because he was forced to focus on me and my needs, and it helped calm my heart and mind and slowly built trust.

We would also both unpack after the counseling sessions, which began almost immediately after the affair. He would come home and talk about what he discussed in counseling. He shared what he was thinking and feeling. During this time, we really shared an intimacy that was beautiful because we both just shared from our hearts. We were both very transparent and it was refreshing to see us growing and healing.

I heard a story of a family going through a similar challenge where the wife, after finding out about her husband's affair with a coworker, would always send one of their children to work with the husband on Saturdays. The children hated going, but she made sure one of them went with him every week. Week after week, the kids took turns going to work with their dad. You would eventually run out of kids and you are essentially putting off the inevitable. This is an extreme that I'm glad I didn't reach, but I can totally see her point. I'm sure she felt better having someone there with him, but it didn't do anyone any good because she would have to trust him on his own eventually.

Brian and I started doing a lot of things together. Grocery shopping had always been my pleasure (sarcasm) but he started going with me. When I shop, I throw things in the cart and move on. He, on the other hand, organizes every bit of everything in the cart and then again on the conveyor belt in the checkout lane. I love spending time with Brian, but let's just say I'm glad to grocery shop alone again.

My point is that we started doing a lot more together. We would drop the kids off places together or run and get dessert together. We would take walks together and do things we had not done together. Ever. This was a huge jolt to Sidney because she was often my partner in errand running. She and I would do a lot together, and when this happened she felt somewhat misplaced.

Brian worked really hard to rebuild relationships with all of the kids, but it was most difficult with Sidney. A year after this happened, they decided they were going to become soccer referees. They got the book and studied the material. They went to class and passed their tests. Brian and Sidney started refereeing games together and would often come home with crazy parent stories from their games. I think this was an integral part of solidifying their relationship because it was "theirs and theirs alone."

One of the major things I would focus on and still do for that matter, is to hold on to what I do know. I don't know if he will cheat again. I don't know if he will leave tomorrow and never come back. What I DO KNOW is that God is good. God loves me. He has me in the palm of His hand. I am hemmed in. I am safe in His arms and in all of this chaos, GOD is in control! Basically, I chose to hang on to what I DO know, and what I DO know is greater than any of my fears.

Time really does help heal. Ecclesiastes 3:11 says it perfectly,

"He has made everything beautiful in its time. Also, he has put eternity into man's heart, yet so that he cannot find out what God has done from the beginning to the end."

He makes all things beautiful in His time. He restores, He heals, He makes all things new.

Literally, each day the trust was rebuilt in small ways, but I had to be aware of it. I had to appreciate the effort Brian was making with both the kids and me intentionally. This was hard some days because I wanted to be in a bad mood or didn't want to give him the credit he deserved for the progress he was making. It was a lot easier to be mad at him most days. I had to be intentional and communicate with him in order for our relationship to grow and heal.

I honestly still struggle occasionally with doubt. I sometimes can't get this other woman out of my head. He hasn't thought of her in years, but I don't think a day goes by without some random thought about her rolling through my head. All that said, I again must be intentional in prayer to get this woman out of my head. This is Satan trying to put doubts in my mind and in my heart to attempt to destroy this marriage. I CAN NOT listen to these doubts. I choose to hang on to what I DO know and what I DO know is greater than any of my doubts!

45

About four and a half years after the affair, I was asked to share in a workshop at a women's retreat. I agreed to this because I know God is calling me to share our story so others see that they are not alone, and that this mountain can be conquered. When I was on the phone I was asked if I had a topic to share, and I was about to say, "Can I get back with you next week?" Instead, out of my mouth came the words, "Rebuilding Trust." I literally didn't know where it came from, but I went with it. The gentleman I was speaking with said it sounded like a great topic that many women would benefit hearing about. I had nothing prepared on this topic or any other topic for that matter. Well, we got off the phone and I said, "Ok Lord! You have to write it too!" And He did!

These steps are not the end all of rebuilding trust. There are many other helpful ways to rebuild trust in relationships. These are just what God laid on my heart to share and they nicely spell out TRUST.

Step One: TURN YOUR EYES TO ME **"Trust in the LORD with all your heart and lean not on your own understanding; [6] in all your ways submit to him, and he will make your paths straight."** Proverbs 3:5-6. God's word is alive. Most of us know this verse and probably have it memorized. The amazing truth in these verses speaks volumes to me. What this verse meant to me as I memorized it in the 2nd grade means something so much deeper as I read it today.

God's word is alive and it reaches us where we are in our lives. I wanted to trust my husband again, but I didn't have it in me. I didn't have the strength to rebuild it. I was so tired.

But, what I could do is trust in the one true God. If I trust wholly in Him, He will make my path straight. When I think of the directions or the paths that I could have taken in my despair, I'm so grateful God had other plans. If I had listened to well-meaning friends and acquaintances I would have ended up a real man hater and probably with a few more problems than I already had! Our trust shouldn't be in anyone before God. When my eyes turn to God, He will make me stronger, wiser, and maybe even easier to live with! With my focus on Him, I will be moving toward God and those in relationship with me will be drawn to God as well. God will never betray me. He will never betray you. He will never forsake me. He will never forsake you! Growing stronger in my relationship with God in my sights will allow me to grow in my relationship with my husband.

Does this mean my husband will never betray me again? Does this make me safe in all my relationships? No. This is not a guarantee here on earth, but I'll tell you what it does guarantee: God allows us to go through things in life and His ultimate goal is for us to draw close to Him. This is a guarantee that God will never forget us. We will not be alone in our journey. EVER! STEP ONE: TURN YOUR EYES TO ME

Step Two: RESPONSIBILITY – HIS NOT OURS, Vengeance is Mine says the Lord! **"Never take your own revenge, beloved, but leave room for the wrath *of God*, for it is written, "Vengeance is Mine, I will repay," says the Lord."** Romans 12:19

I love how the Message translation shares this passage**: "Don't hit back; discover beauty in everyone. If you've got it in you, get along with everybody. Don't insist on getting even; that's not for you to do. 'I'll do the judging,' says God. 'I'll take care of it."**

Can I get an Amen? Nothing I could do, nothing I could dream up, nothing I could create in my sick mind in the middle of a sleepless night could come close to what God has in store for those who betrayed my trust. I am a child of the one true God. He will avenge me. NOTHING I could dream up could come close. I have to give this up to God, sometimes every day.

I sometimes get this picture of God intently listening to me. He's answering my questions with patience and I have all of His attention, but when I bring this up, "Lord how are you going to deal with that woman? What about my husband?" He looks at me and says, "Don't you worry your pretty little head about it! I've got this."

And not in a demeaning way, not condescending, but sincerely He says, "I've got this taken care of." He wants me to get on with the great work of healing. He doesn't want me to stoop to a nasty level so that he has to forgive me too. Step Two: RESPONSIBILITY – HIS NOT OURS

Step Three: UTTERLY FORGOTTEN Ephesians 4:31-32 **"Get rid of all bitterness, rage and anger, brawling and slander, along with every form of malice. Be kind and compassionate to one another, forgiving each other, just as in Christ God forgave you."** What a laundry list, this is! Bitterness, rage, anger, brawling, slander, not a small one in the group! Nothing is left out!

Stop the history lesson. Let it go! They know what they did. Do not bring up the past and throw it in their face every chance you get. This produces nothing but more misery. I'm the queen of sarcasm and one liners. Believe me, if sarcasm was a spiritual gift, I wouldn't even need to take the test to figure it out. I have done a bunch of tongue biting. But listen to me. DO MORE TONGUE BITING THAN TONGUE WAGGING! Life is too short and precious.

Compassion goes so much further than bitterness, and think of the example to those around you. Your children need to see and hear you uplifting your spouse. Especially when talking about him to other people, get rid of all slander, bitterness, rage, anger. Hold him up! Talk with compassion and kindness to him and to others about him.

Ok, side note: I love the word UTTERLY. It makes me laugh. I have an older sister, and when we were growing up we belonged to a public pool called Meineke Pool in Schaumburg, Illinois. Every summer we would get these little metal tags to show that we were members, and my mom would safety pin the tag to our swimsuits. It's what we did along with every other kid in the pool. Well, my sister, Judi, had a friend visiting for a few days and she broke her ankle playing who knows what in the back yard. My mom took her to get an x-ray and since she needed to get a cast put on my mom decided to take Laura, my sister's friend, and I to the pool while Judi went to get her cast. We had guest passes but couldn't find them, at the moment, so my mom took the tag off of Judi's swimsuit and pinned it to Laura's swimsuit. We waited in line and when the lady checked our tags she said to Laura, "No. This pass is not yours." I, as a second grader, said, "Well, my sister broke her ankle and this is our friend and we couldn't find the guest pass but my mom is taking my sister to get her cast put on." She said, "No. You can't swim today." So we went out to the parking lot where my mom was waiting to make sure we could get in. We told her what the lady said and my mom, who really didn't anger easily, marched us back to the entrance of the pool and explained the situation to the lady. But, the lady was having none of this and she said, "Well, you can pay for her to swim today." And my mom said, "Come on, girls! SOME PEOPLE ARE UTTERLY IMPOSSIBLE!" I can't see the word utterly without laughing about that moment. We still laugh about that day. And I do realize it has very little to do with this point, except for the strength of the word UTTERLY!

Forgive as He forgave you. I realize this is a revolving door some days. Keep walking towards forgiveness over and over again. Remind yourself how YOU are forgiven and free. Now, trust me when I say you won't forget--I totally get that. Make sure your spouse knows that the past feels like it is utterly forgotten. Don't be ignorant about it. I'm not saying be a doormat, but be gracious with the past. Move in the right direction. You alone hold the power to stop the history lesson. Step Three: UTTERLY FORGOTTEN

Step Four: SLATE WIPED CLEAN **"Purify me from my sins and I will be clean; wash me, and I will be whiter than snow. Oh, give me back my joy again; you have broken me—now let me rejoice. Don't keep looking at my sins. Remove the stain of my guilt. Create in me a clean heart, O God. Renew a loyal spirit within me."** Psalm 51:7-10

I loved the opportunity of being a coordinator of our MOPS group and it never felt like work. But, there were times when we'd be setting up on a Thursday night for the MOPS meeting the next morning and as hormonal, sleep deprived, up to our eyes in dirty diapers young moms, there would be melt downs and petty arguments that would occur on occasion. My prayer every MOPS meeting was that God would allow me to see these women on the Steering Team and the women in the group, with His eyes. I would ask that God would give me a "Clean Slate" so I could love them fully and encourage them in whatever they were facing. We certainly didn't solve all of our problems, but I believe from the bottom of my heart that this simple prayer allowed our ministry to avoid a bus load of explosive issues that could have potentially brought down, as well as the women we were serving through this ministry.

So, CLEAN SLATE your husband. CLEAN SLATE your children. CLEAN SLATE your neighbor. This simple process of pleading with the Lord helped me to clean slate my husband so I didn't lash out at him. He will answer this prayer. Hear me, GOD will ALWAYS answer this prayer! He will allow you that glimpse of what He sees in your spouse. Your spouse is just as forgiven as you are! Step Four: SLATE WIPED CLEAN

Step Five: TREASURED! Nahum 1:7 **"The Lord is good, a refuge in times of trouble. He cares for those who trust in Him."**

In the Old Testament book of Nahum, the prophet speaks of the vision he had regarding Ninevah. The vision is all about the wrath of God and how God is slow to anger, but now, basically he's saying, "Time's up!" The vengeance of the Lord is coming now. Verses 1-6 in chapter 1 describe His wrath as it continues to build.

"The oracle of Nineveh. The book of the vision of Nahum the Elkoshite.

A jealous and avenging God is the LORD;
The LORD is avenging and wrathful.
The LORD takes vengeance on His adversaries,
And He reserves wrath for His enemies.
The LORD is slow to anger and great in power,
And the LORD will by no means leave *the guilty* unpunished.
In whirlwind and storm is His way,
And clouds are the dust beneath His feet.

He rebukes the sea and makes it dry;
He dries up all the rivers.
Bashan, and Carmel wither;
The blossoms of Lebanon wither.

Mountains quake because of Him
And the hills dissolve;
Indeed the earth is upheaved by His presence,
The world and all the inhabitants in it.

Who can stand before His indignation?
Who can endure the burning of His anger?
His wrath is poured out like fire
And the rocks are broken up by Him.

The LORD is good,
A stronghold in the day of trouble,
And He knows those who take refuge in Him. He knows those
who TRUST in Him!!!!

But with an overflowing flood
He will make a complete end of its site,
And will pursue His enemies into darkness."

Verse 7 says right in the middle of this tirade, **"The Lord is good, He is a good God a just God. He is a refuge in times of trouble. He cares for those who trust in Him, He knows who you are! If you trust in Him, He knows you and you are safe. He will shelter you."** Then, in verse 8 it's back to: **"But with an overflowing flood He will make a complete end of its site, and will pursue His enemies into darkness."**

Again, I am not a theologian, but this little "by the way" in verse 7 is so refreshing. It's like a clue to the extra credit on your big test. Like God is saying here is what's going down, but "hint - hint, check out verse 7... I'm giving you another look at the answer... hint - hint."

He will bring shelter to those who trust in Him. You are treasured by him if you trust in him, he KNOWS you. You are His treasure! What an amazing promise. Again, this is not a guarantee that bad things won't come your way, but a promise that He's got you covered. Step Five: TREASURED! He cares for those who trust in Him. You will not be forgotten!

46

This is a letter that our daughter, Sidney, wrote regarding her journey through this time in our lives:

Growing up as a pastor's kid has its perks, everyone knows your family, you are always allowed to get into anything at the church (mainly the gym), you also tend to be, dare I say, popular. I always enjoyed being able to take advantage of these perks. Even though I knew that was not the sole reason I should be attending church.

When my dad decided to have his affair, I was devastated. I hated him, I didn't want anything to do with him or anyone who thought he was still a "great guy". I ran (literally) from every opportunity I had to hang out with him for years. This whole father daughter bond was non-existent. I became jealous and irritated at every father daughter interaction I would see my friends have. I would cry and practically scream every time my mom told me I should go help my dad in the yard or run to get some milk from the store with him.

Before this whole thing happened my dad and my relationship wasn't exactly perfect, we disagreed, we didn't spend much time together.

Even though my dad was trying to fix his relationship with my mom it didn't seem like he wanted to fix what he had broken between us. It felt like I was kicked to the side. This then led to many thoughts and things I did to myself and others.

Throughout my freshman and sophomore years in high school, I was very rebellious and did things that were uncalled for and honestly just to spite my dad. I hated him, I wanted him to feel pain, more pain, I wanted him to go through what I was feeling and hate himself. All that ended up happening was me falling into a deeper hatred towards myself.

Throughout my high school career, I became bitter, closed off, evil, all because of what my dad had done. I had put him on a pedestal and I had made what he had done something I wanted to dwell on. I always thought to myself, "He's a pastor, how could he do this?" At the end of my senior year and throughout my first year of college, I grew, a lot. I matured and I learned a lot of lessons. I also realized that Satan was behind all of this crap. Once I became aware of this I stopped everything and made a 180.

Throughout my freshman year of college, I had this ongoing thing with two of my friends. After first semester, we told ourselves (mainly them telling me) that we are turning over a new leaf. This new leaf meant that we will be getting better grades, focusing on positive things, not gawking over boys (which quickly got removed from the list.) But, with my new leaf it had a deeper meaning. I realized that I need to change my mind set with my dad. I needed to forgive and forget just as God does with us. This took a lot of willpower and many nights filled with tears, and Scripture, fighting the idea that I need to love my dad and forgive him. As my freshman year of college came to a close I realized with the help of my mom and close friends that God had truly been working in my life that year and that even though I thought I wasn't taking a step forward, God was making strides for me. Even if our relationship isn't what I want it to be I know that I have a heavenly Father who adores me more than anyone on this earth.

I got a tattoo this summer much to my parents' dismay. I had been wanting one for a while and finally got the guts to get it. I was throwing a bunch of options around in my head, but the one that never changed was the two words, "Hemmed In." Psalms 139:5-6 says, "You hem me in, behind and before, and you lay your hand upon me. Such knowledge is too wonderful for me, too lofty for me to attain." This verse means so much to me and my daily walk with Christ. The struggle of having family issues and being a young adult is tough, but knowing you are hemmed in everyday is a good reminder that God is always there. God's knowledge is too wonderful for me and His plan is so much greater than mine.

--Sidney Clay

47

If you would have asked me what I would do if Brian cheated on me six months before it happened, I would probably have told you I would leave. We would be over. Well, then it happened and my response surprised even me. Please don't take this the wrong way but I think at the time, divorce would have been the easy way out. I could have turned off feelings and not had to fight through the mess and muck to preserve our family. I know divorce is never easy. It's awful and heart wrenching.

It might have been easier to walk away and start fresh, lick my wounds and pick up the pieces. I would somehow try to shut off my feelings for him. Trying to juggle the kids and make two homes for them would have been devastating. It would have been heart wrenching to watch Brian date someone else God forbid, marry her and even worse, to have the kids like her. It is still hard to comprehend what he did during our marriage let alone the freedom he would feel to do whatever after our marriage ended. I can barely go there in my head while I'm writing this right now.

God is so good. He saw us through an extremely dark time in our lives. He is faithful. He is strong. I look at Brian today and I'm grateful for the journey. Will we have bad times ahead? Of course we will. But with the history we have shared, I believe whatever comes our way we can weather the storm together. I wonder sometimes what our lives would be like if Brian had not made those bad decisions back in 2011. Although I'm not happy to have gone through that mess, I'm grateful for the people we have become on this side of it.

I pray for him every day to be the man that God wants him to be. Instead of begging God to make Brian into the husband and father that I want him to be, I pray that he will honor God with his choices and the rest will fall into place. I've always loved Brian, but I love him with a different awareness these days. I love him more intentionally. Does he still drive me crazy mad sometimes? Well, of course he does. But we face issues differently. We are not perfect at this marriage thing, but we don't take anything for granted anymore.

He is preaching at our home church and in area churches again, and I'm so proud of him. I used to see unwavering strength when he would preach. Now I see this overwhelming sense of vulnerability in Brian, and it makes me even more proud. It was not just us who fought to stay together, to fight for our marriage…. It was God in us.

48

I am forever grateful for the love, concern, and mostly the prayers of all our friends and acquaintances. Thank you for your kindness and your prayers. I know our God answers prayer. Thank you for investing time in praying for us.

In conclusion, I want to talk to a few different groups of people. First, those who have cheated. You know what damage you have done in your relationships. You made horrible choices, selfish choices. The good news is that our God is a loving, forgiving God. You are His child and although He weeps for you and with you, He alone will give you the strength and the tools to fight for your family. He will heal you and your relationships if you allow Him to.

Put healthy boundaries in place to prevent these messes in the future. Cherish your relationships. Listen to your spouse. Let them set the pace for healing. Do not rush them. This is about them healing. Give them the grace they deserve to grieve your past relationship and start building again. Focus on growing closer to God and to those you are committed to first. Make this a priority. Fight for your marriage. He is a forgiving God and He can make all things new.

Those of you have been cheated on: You are hemmed in. You are a child of God and He will never betray you. He will never forget you. He is trustworthy. You are loved, cherished and adored. If you are in an abusive relationship, DO NOT STAY. If you are in danger, DO NOT STAY. However, if both of you are willing and open to work on your relationship, by all means work on it. God is so powerful. It may look like a mountain in front of you right now but trust me when I say that God will help you with every step. EVERY SINGLE STEP. Pray like you've never prayed before. Lean on Him. Grow in your knowledge of God's Word. Communicate with each other. Encourage your spouse. Healthy healing is possible.

To the family and friends of couples going through this, please first and foremost - PRAY. Hit your knees for these people. God will give you wisdom, and remember that you don't need details. God knows and that's enough. Simply let the couple know you are praying. If they need to talk, they will. Just let them know you are willing to walk beside them and listen. Do not ask probing questions. They will share when they feel like it. Just please pray.

To churches and ministries: Just like you have a fire escape plan in your building, you need a plan if you don't already have one to help couples rebuild their relationships. Your church most likely has an outline for you to follow when a couple comes into the church wanting to have their wedding there. You follow that outline or checklist with their requests and needs for that special day. What about when you have a death in your congregation? There is an outline or checklist available to help plan the funeral, times, place, pastoral needs, special music, right?

So, I'm begging you. If you don't already have a plan in place in your church or ministry, please put one together. I realize every situation is different, and not every story has a happy ending, but if you start the process of healthy healing early on you have no idea how many marriages may be saved. If you lay down the ground work to start both individuals on a path to healing, praise God. Our plan included individual counseling at the beginning. We had amazing counselors that helped us immensely. Have a list ready of Christian marriage counselors in your area, and they, most likely, will greatly assist you as you set up a restoration process for your church or ministry. Help your church fight for their marriages. We are all in this together.

"Come, let us sing to the Lord! Let us shout joyfully to the Rock of our salvation. Let us come to him with thanksgiving. Let us sing psalms of praise to him. For the Lord is a great God, a great King above all gods. He holds in his hands the depths of the earth and the mightiest mountains. The sea belongs to him, for he made it. His hands formed the dry land, too. Come, let us worship and bow down. Let us kneel before the Lord our maker, for he is our God.

We are the people he watches over, the flock under his care. If only you would listen to his voice today!"

Psalm 95: 1-7

Works Cited

BibleGateway.com
.com: A Searchable Online Bible in over 150 Versions and 50 Languages. N.p.,
n.d. Web. Feb.-Mar. 2016. <https://www.biblegateway.com/>.

"It's Your Life," Francesca Battistelli
Battistelli, Francesca. *This Is Your Life*. By Francesca Battestelli and Ian Eskelin.
Francesca Battistelli. Ian Eskelin, 2008. *AZlyrics.com*. Web.
<http://www.azlyrics.com/lyrics/francescabattistelli/itsyourlife.html>.

Torn Asunder by David Carder
Carder, David, and Duncan Jaenicke. *Torn Asunder: Recovering from
Extramarital Affairs*. Chicago: Moody, 1995. Print.

"Worn," by Tenth Avenue North
Donehey, Mike. By Jeff Owen, Mike Donehey, and Jason Ingram. *Worn*. Tenth
Avenue North. Jason Ingram, 2012. *AZlyrics.com*. Web. Feb.-Mar. 2016.
<http://www.azlyrics.com/lyrics/tenthavenuenorth/worn.html>.

Broom, Al, and Lorraine Broom. *One-to-one Discipling: A 9-lesson Study to
Be Used by One Person to Disciple Another*. Vista, CA: Multiplication
Ministries, 1987. Print.

Batterson, Mark. "In a Pit With a Lion on a Snowy Day." *LifeWay: Your
Source for Bible Studies, Christian Books, Bibles, and More...* N.p., n.d. Web.
07 Nov. 2016. <http://www.lifeway.com/Product/in-a-pit-with-a-lion-on-a-
snowy-day-P001311932>.

Batterson, Mark. *The Circle Maker: Praying Circles around Your Biggest
Dreams and Greatest Fears*. Grand Rapids, MI: Zondervan, 2011. Print.

Made in the USA
Lexington, KY
14 May 2017